A Woma

The Tangled Web

Dr. Luauna Stines

A Woman Called of God

The Tangled Web

This book is based on a true story, some names have been changed

All scripture quotations are from: Spirit Filled Life Bible
Copyright © 1991 by Thomas Nelson, Inc.
New King James Version of the Bible
&
Authorized King James Version
Red Letter Edition

ISBN: 978-0-9884172-9-8

Printed in the U.S.A. by
LS Publishing
P.O. Box 2800
Ramona, CA 92065

A Woman Called of God

The Tangled Web

Dr. Luauna Stines

LS Publishing

FOREWORD

A Woman Called of God – The Tangled Web has taken a long time to come to print. When we're off-balance, we experience great pain in every area of our daily life. I bare my soul with the hope of helping millions of men and women to understand why finding balance is so important.

Balance is more precious than gold.

We can live a balanced life today in an unbalanced world. Take courage; it is possible!

We must remove the invisible "burqa" of religious traditions and prejudice, which has held women in captivity, and left many men broken and hurting, even in the Christian church.

One day while walking out my door, as I approached the end of my walkway, the morning dew had fallen, and mist outlined an amazing spider web. I stood and looked at the web; it was astounding; I saw the skeletons of bugs, some dried up, others still trapped, and some trying to escape the hold of this spider's web.

I realized, like the spider that deliberately spun its web to capture its prey, the enemy of my soul- the devil- had done the same thing. The plan was to destroy, to suck the life out of my future and me. This started at a young age, when I'd been dropped off at an orphanage. From that moment, at every turn, the odds were stacked against me. But JESUS came and delivered me out of Satan's web of destruction. *Rise up Valiant Warrior- RISE UP!*

Dr. Luauna Stines

RECOMMENDATION

It is a privilege to recommend Dr. Luauna Stines' ministry and affirm her personal Christian life for ministry. Several healings have followed her preaching that I know of, and possibly many more that I do not know of. Fervency and an anointing of the Holy Spirit are earmarks of her ministry.

It seems apparent that the Holy Spirit has been silently grooming her for a greater ministry because of her strong love for the unsaved. In the meantime, I have been grateful to see results wherever she has preached. Through her ministry, many casual believers have been stirred to seek God for their personal Christian growth and development.

Dr. Stines has an outstanding personal testimony that she shares when the Holy Spirit prompts her to share it. She is a living example of the tremendous grace of God.

I believe the Holy Spirit will leave His mark on the churches where she has ministered. I commend her to you and trust that in God's time your church will have the privilege of her ministry.

Sincerely in Christ,

Lydia Swain (Mrs.)
Former Director of Foreign Affairs and Ministries
for Dr. David Yonggi Cho (13 years)
Yoido Full Gospel Church, Seoul, Korea

FOREWORD

Revelation 12:11 says, "And they overcame him by the blood of the Lamb, and by the word of their testimony; and they loved not their lives unto the death." Of all books that I have read, Dr. Luauna Stines book, entitled <u>A Woman Called of God – The Tangled Web</u>, epitomizes the truth of this scripture.

Dr. Stines' book does not hide her alcohol and drug-centered life as a youth, her reform school experiences, and her many fights; but it also is inspirational when her life changed going into a small church and finding her Savior, Christ Jesus. Her book compels you to turn to the next page and keep reading. In her youth, no one thought that Dr. Stines would amount to anything worthwhile. Yet, the Lord usually looks into the junk yards, the trash heaps, and the dumpsters for the rejected ones to choose as His servants.

One day the Lord looked into the heart of a young teenage girl sitting next to a trash bin near the restaurant where she had been working waiting for her ride home and found an Apostle to anoint for His Majesty's service. That very night she had to fight off a would-be rapist. When Dr. Stines found Jesus, she also found a close friend in church that stood with her. The Lord miraculously delivered her from her drug addiction, and she continued her life-changing journey being led by the Holy Spirit, trusting the Lord that He had a wonderful plan for her life.

Just because she was chosen by the Lord as His minister did not mean there would be no more tragedies in her life. It did not mean her struggles were over, even though they may have taken a different means of warfare or a different venue. It did not mean there would be no more financial difficulties. Similarly, instructing him to visit Saul on a street called Straight, the Lord said to Ananias, "For I will shew him how great things he must suffer for my name's sake" (Acts 9:16). Paul's call of suffering seems to be a similar ministry call of Dr. Stines.

Later, in Philippians 3:10, Paul said that the main purpose of his calling was: "That I may know Him, and the power of His resurrection, and the fellowship of His sufferings, being made conformable unto His death." I found this same overriding testimony in Dr. Stines' book. In Christ Jesus she had found the One whom her heart was searching her entire young life, and she has given Him her all since then. She has suffered more than her share of tragedies, but with the Holy Spirit's loving guidance and assurance, she has overcome them all. She is truly a mature woman of God.

Dr. Stines' book, <u>A Woman Called of God-The Tangled Web</u>, is full of faith that overcomes the circumstances encountered in this world, and testifies of the resilience of a woman truly called of God. Dr. Stines' book is a deep insightful journey through the life of a lowly rebellious young woman that was transformed into the likeness of her Savior, so she could be His servant and loving companion. Her sharing of her own life's journey is an illumination of the spiritual dynamics taking place in God's unseen, spiritual world for the importance of the transformation of a single soul for the populating of His Kingdom here on earth.

Dr. Stines' book, <u>A Woman Called of God-The Tangled Web</u>, is a must read for not only women, but for all believers who have been discredited, marginalized, and rejected as inferior in quality by those in the world. Dr. Stine's book is especially relevant to young people who have been dismissed as unworthy, been labeled as a failure, been condemned as a rebellious youth, and been counted as incorrigible. Her testimony gives hope to the hopeless, and encouragement to those lost in their own iniquities. By the words of Dr. Stines own testimony in her book, you can experience

A Woman Called of God

encouragement that you, too, can overcome, be victorious, and be used of the Lord for a great work.

Dr. Nova Dean Pack
Christian International Embassy Ministries
Christian Attorney at law, (since 1974)
Colton, CA

ABOUT THE AUTHOR

Dr. Luauna Stines is the Founder and President of A Touch From Above, LSM Inc. Her goal is to reach a world of hurting people with her story of God's amazing grace. Through hard life trials: a childhood of rejection, a forced marriage at the age of 15, a murdered husband, betrayal of marriage, and the loss of everything she had worked for...there emerged an inspiring testimony of hope and victory, a drastic change in Dr. Stines' life when she had a collision with the truth of the Gospel of Jesus Christ.

She is the author of *A Mother's Story, Mission America, Golden Nuggets*, and now *A Woman Called of God: The Tangled Web*.

As a minister for over 35 years, Dr. Stines received an honorary doctorate from the I.M.I. Bible College and Seminary, and District Ministerial License from LIFE Bible College of the International Church of the Foursquare Gospel. She also holds an education certificate in Ministry Training and Development from Oral Roberts University.

Dr. Stines is an apostle, evangelist, teacher, preacher, and pastor. She has preached the Gospel throughout the world in parts of the former Yugoslavia, Italy, England, Germany, Switzerland, Central Africa, Korea, Australia, Mexico, and the United States. In her travels, she has also preached for the satellite churches of Dr. Yonggi Cho of the Yoido Full Gospel Church in Seoul, Pusan, Chonju and Inchon, located in South Korea.

Preaching on television in San Diego, California, Dr. Stines touches the hearts of thousands with a simple pure message, "When You Are Hardest Hit, Don't Quit." A Touch From Above- Dr. Luauna Stines, also ministers on radio every Sunday morning at 8 a.m. on KPRZ 1210 AM in San Diego. To listen live, go to kprz.com, click: LISTEN LIVE.

She is the founder of Victorious Homes for Men and Women, a discipleship program. Over 500 men and women have come through the program over the past 20 years in Colorado and Oregon.

Dr. Stines is building A Touch From Above- Prayer Mountain, located in Ramona, California. In the heart of San Diego County, 25 acres of land have been set aside for God's people to pray and trust God to answer all their needs, and lead them into their God-given call. Prayer works! She also preaches every Sunday at the Prayer Mountain, to train and equip men and women for God's service.

Dr. Luauna Stines is now preparing online, "A Touch From Above- Christian University", for training and launching men and women into the harvest field of the world, to preach the Gospel of Jesus Christ.

After returning from Seoul, Korea with a burden in her heart, "We need a place for God's people to pray in the USA," she knew it would take great faith for the walls of prayer to be rebuilt in America. Not just a whisper, but the "effective, fervent prayer of a righteous man or woman that availeth much." The Prayer Mountain is now being built; ministers and saints alike are coming to seek the Lord in prayer.

She is a weekly columnist appearing in the East County Gazette. Her website is www.atouchfromabove.org

Dr. Luauna Stines is the mother of two children, now grown.

WHY YOU SHOULD READ THIS BOOK

Does it seem like you're trapped in a snare of hopelessness? Have the odds been stacked against you at every turn and you don't know what to do? My heart is burdened to help those who are broken and in a state of despair. I have seen, over the years, this deep hurt plague so many. Read my story, and you will see how to find your way out of distress.

Psalms 1:1-3: "Blessed is the man who walks not in the counsel of the ungodly, nor stands in the path of sinners, nor sits in the seat of the scornful; but his delight is in the law of the Lord, and in His law he meditates day and night. He shall be like a tree planted by the rivers of water that brings forth its fruit in its season, whose leaf also shall not wither; and whatever he does shall prosper."

If you are one of those powerful women whom God is calling, and have experienced opposition, this book will encourage and inspire you to stand strong for Jesus. Our enemy, the devil, has placed invisible chains, and an invisible burqa on the other half of God's army, the women. You will be free in Christ to fulfill the Lord's purpose for your life.

Galatians 3:28: "There is neither Jew nor Greek, there is neither slave nor free, there is neither male nor female; for you are all one in Christ Jesus."

DEDICATION

This book is dedicated with my whole heart to Jesus Christ, my Lord and Savior and the Holy Spirit who walked with me in the deepest, darkest trials of my life.

Thank you to all those powerful, amazing men of God: pastors, husbands, and sons whom I have met throughout the years, who have a true understanding of God's call on women. Thank you for supporting, loving, and encouraging these women of God as the *life giver*, great is your reward in heaven.

For those men, husbands, and sons who have been guilty of calling God's amazing daughters, "Jezebels", women who have been called by the Holy Spirit, I have a word from the Lord for you: "Do not call unclean, what the Lord has cleansed." Remember one day you WILL give an account of every WORD you have spoken.

James 3:9-10: "With it we bless our God and Father, and with it we curse men, who have been made in the similitude of God. Out of the same mouth proceed blessing and cursing. My brethren, these things ought not to be so."

Even those who told me I was "nothing, not called, shut up, sit down, or get married." Thank you, because I have learned to rightly divide the Word, and discovered the right balance. Without you I might not be where I am today. I am *A Woman Called of God,* and I do love you too.

TABLE OF CONTENTS

CREATED IN HIS IMAGE

1

Genesis 1:26-31: "And God said, 'Let us make man in our image, after our likeness: and let them have dominion over the fish of the sea, and over the fowl of the air, and over the cattle, and over all the earth, and over every creeping thing that creepeth upon the earth.' So God created man in his own image, in the image of God created he him; male and female created he them. And God blessed them, and God said unto them, 'Be fruitful, and multiply, and replenish the earth, and subdue it: and have dominion over the fish of the sea, and over the fowl of the air, and over every living thing that moveth upon the earth.' And God said, 'Behold, I have given you every herb bearing seed, which is upon the face of all the earth, and every tree, in the which is the fruit of a tree yielding seed; to you it shall be for meat. And to every beast of the earth, and to every fowl of the air, and to everything that creepeth upon the earth, wherein there is life, I have given every green herb for meat:' and it was so. And God saw everything that he had made, and, behold, it was very good. And the evening and the morning were the sixth day."

First, I want to thank you for taking your valuable time out to read my book. This book has been a long time coming; since I

have gone through many trials and fire, I write "A Woman Called of God - The Tangled Web."

When I first walked into a church, I had never been to any church. I guess I was the one whom people would call "a good old sinner." I never had a Bible growing up, nor did I know scriptures, but one thing I did know, the morning I walked into that little Victorian 1898 white building trimmed in brown, it was a sight to behold!

The inside was breathtaking, complete with ornate wood décor; the wood panels and beautifully carved arches on the ceiling were truly eye catching. Its exquisite stained glass windows let the morning sun shine in with brilliant colors, of red, yellow and blues. This little corner church had stood stoically nestled on the corner for many years, right in the heart of the city of Colorado Springs, Colorado. With a background of the snowcapped Rocky Mountains, and Pikes Peak sitting majestically right in the middle, it looked like a picture on a postcard.

The day I walked into that little church would change my life forever. Not knowing what was done in church, I mustered enough courage and walked in through those doors, nervous as a cat walking on the top of a hot tin roof. A very kind gentleman named Ted walked up to me. I'm sure he knew I had never been to church, by the way I looked around and of course my style of dressing was not quite the norm for church attendance. He smiled, looked me right in the eyes and asked if I needed a seat. I almost turned and walked out but his sweet and gentle kindness kept me following him as he led me to a seat in a place that was called the mezzanine.

That morning I was coming off cocaine; my nerves were jumping and I needed just one line of cocaine-or so I thought! -

but after Ted sat me in a place where I would have to walk in front of everyone to go to the bathroom, I was too shy and insecure to want to get up once I was seated.

I thought to myself, "If I can just make it through this church service, I'll be OK"- I would go out to my car and do a line of cocaine afterwards, but God had *another* plan!

That morning, something hit my heart deep. Something strange was pulling at my heart; I'd never felt this before. I felt vulnerable, I wanted to run out of the church, but it was like I was frozen in the seat. The preacher asked everyone to bow their heads. I followed everyone's lead, yet I wanted to see what was happening; after all, I had never been to church. I covered my face with my hands over my eyes, but I lifted my head up a little bit to see. The preacher said, "You are here, you're a sinner!" Right then I wondered, "What is a sinner?" I kept looking to see who or what a sinner was. As I looked around peeking through my fingers, I looked up at the preacher, and he was pointing right at me. "You tried everything, why don't you give Jesus a chance?" My eyes must have been opened as big as saucers; right then I put my head down and covered up my eyes.

Something was happening; I had a pulling inside of my heart, a tugging, yet there was a war going on inside. That pulling was strong, and before I knew what I was doing, I walked forward. To this day, I still don't remember what the sermon was, or how I ended up standing there in the front of the church. I just stood there; to my right and left, others were coming forward. The preacher said, "Jesus wants to be your Lord, pray, ask Him to come into your heart!" I stood there looking around. I didn't know how or what to pray, as I'd never prayed before. As I was standing, I could feel this nervous feeling coming over me, and then all of a sudden this redheaded young woman walked up beside me. She smiled and with her soft, gentle voice told me her name was Mary. She was kind, and spoke sweetly! I had a fleeting thought: "She must be faking it, being so kind." I'd never heard someone speak to me with such tenderness. With a sparkle in her eye, she asked me, "Can I pray with you?"

Looking right back at her, I replied, "I don't know how to pray."

"No problem, I'll help you." We knelt down and she asked me to repeat a simple, little prayer, and before I knew it, I said, "Amen!"

Mary smiled at me, but something was happening inside.

That day I answered my first altar call, walking up to the front of that little church and looking down at the violet red carpet; I knelt down and said a simple prayer, which would change my whole life. I cried for days. I didn't really understand all that was happening to me, but I was different inside. I couldn't stop the tears. Twelve other people gave their hearts to Jesus that morning; we all did the same thing. Here I was, kneeling down and praying with someone I had never met before. After rising from the altar, we were then ushered into a back room while the man who'd given the invitation stood and gently smiled at all of us.

I tried to hide; I saw a seat behind everyone who was standing, so I sat down. I didn't want anyone to see me weeping, because I couldn't hold back the tears. I hadn't cried since my husband's death. I really wanted to cry out loud like a baby who had just fallen down. I was shocked, it was like a flood of tears had been trapped inside of me forever and ever; now they wanted to escape and erupt like a volcano. I was trying hard to keep my composure, but it was hard. We were all asked if we had a Bible, and when the man looked at me and asked me point blank, "Do you have a Bible?" I shook my head no.

He then reached through the people and handed me a new Bible. I looked at it, still trying to hold back the tears. I didn't know what was happening to me. I hadn't cried for so many years.

In that back room, the man said, "What you did this morning is real; you gave your life to Jesus Christ." He continued sharing with us, "The key to help in your walk with the Lord is to be in church every time those doors are open." I asked him for a schedule; I think I threw him off guard! He found something written with the services and times, then said goodbye to everyone, and asked us to fill out a little white card before we left. I didn't have a pen, and after a while they collected all the cards except mine. I placed mine in my Bible and walked out the side door.

I wanted to get to my car because something was still happening inside me. I started up my car, and drove about two or three blocks down the street, then pulled over because I couldn't see through all the tears. I leaned my head over on the steering wheel and –BAM! - the tears wouldn't stop; they kept flowing like a river. I wept like a baby for what seemed forever, a very long time. I didn't know what was happening inside. But there was something different about me. Looking for a Kleenex to wipe my nose and eyes, I finally pulled myself together enough to drive home.

When I got home, my two children greeted me. Kaweah, my daughter, was only 4 years old, and son Samuel was 6. I sat down on a chair and the tears started up again. My kids were very tender in heart, and approached me with concern. Samuel touched the tears running down my face with his finger; he asked, "Mommy, what's wrong? Why are you crying?"

I didn't know how to explain it to them, they were so young. I didn't know how to describe it to myself. I gave them both a big hug and told them, "We're going to start going to church."

Each day the church had a service I was there. You couldn't keep me out of church with a thousand horses. I sat towards the back of the church for the first couple of years because I was very shy and insecure. Most of the time, I would sit up in the balcony with my two kids.

This church thing was new to me, when the preacher would tell us where to open our Bibles I would get lost. I finally figured out there was an index at the front of this book called the Bible. I didn't want anyone to know I didn't know where to find the different books in the Bible.

After a few weeks I remember going into the thrift store, and as I passed the books, I noticed a whole bunch of Bibles. "Wow," I thought, "I hit the jack pot!" I rolled a shopping cart over, and started to fill it up with all kinds of Bibles. Children's Bibles, New International Version, New King James, the Student Bible, even one done in all comic form, and the Living Bible. Then I realized I could not understand some of the words, I looked for a dictionary. I noticed a Strong's Bible Concordance, and I was set. When I arrived home I set my newfound treasures carefully upon one half of the table and told the kids, "Please do not play with Mom's new books."

To better understand, I started bringing a notebook to church and taking notes during every sermon. I was fearful the person sitting next to me would try to read my notes because I was such a bad speller, that I put one child on either side of me, to block my neighbors' view! I wanted to write down every scripture as it was preached, because I couldn't find them in my Bible as quickly as the pastor spoke; I wasn't fast enough. I wrote them all down so when I got home I could take my time and look them up again, reading them over and over until the next service.

Bound and determined to know this new way of living, as I wanted to know this God who touched my heart, I read every day without fail.

I am sharing in detail how I was saved for the purpose of explaining important things you will read later in this book.

FEARFULLY AND WONDERFULLY MADE

2

Psalm 139:13-18;"For thou hast possessed my reins: thou hast covered me in my mother's womb. I will praise thee; for I am fearfully and wonderfully made: marvelous are thy works; and that my soul knoweth right well. My substance was not hid from thee, when I was made in secret, and curiously wrought in the lowest parts of the earth. Thine eyes did see my substance, yet being unperfect; and in thy book all my members were written, which in continuance were fashioned, when as yet there was none of them. How precious also are thy thoughts unto me, O God! How great is the sum of them! If I should count them, they are more in number than the sand: when I awake, I am still with thee."

Something wonderful happened in my life from the first day I walked into the little church, and I didn't want it to stop. Kaweah and Samuel were so cute; I tried to explain to them what had happened to me that morning I gave my heart to Jesus, but they didn't understand, any more than I did! The same day I was saved, after church I went to pull out a cigarette but I stopped right in my tracks. I looked at that cigarette with disgust for the first time. I had been smoking two to three packs a day of Kool Menthol Longs.

I remembered what the man told us in the back room, something about, "Rebuking temptation when it comes to you." I forgot the word, "Rebuke," but I did remember him saying that there was power in the name of Jesus. He shared this with all of us in the back room: "When you say the name of Jesus, the devil gets mad. That name has power!"

I looked at the pack of cigarettes in one hand, and put the cigarette I had taken out of the pack, back into the pack. With both hands I wrung the pack of cigarettes like it were a washrag squeezing as hard as I could with my fingers. I said, "JESUS, Jesus, Jesus, I don't know how to pray but help me right now."

I set the crumbled pack of cigarettes right on top of my fridge. I stood them up so I could see them every time I walked into the kitchen. For three months I said, "Jesus, thank you for helping me not smoke."

At the end of the third month I laughed, reached up and said, "HA, HA devil," and threw the crumbled pack of cigarettes in the trash. By God's grace, I never smoked another cigarette from that day on.

The same afternoon after lunch, I reached into the cabinets and threw away all my liquor. I stood in front of the sink and dumped them down the drain. Then I remembered I had one gram of cocaine in a small vial bottle. I ran to my bag, opened it, and threw the white powder down the drain. Then I remembered I had a 6 gram vial bottle also filled with cocaine. I ran to get it, opened it and threw it down the drain as well. Over $1,000 worth of drugs went down the drain the very same day I gave my heart to Jesus.

The afternoon was quickly fading away; I reached over to look at the things they gave me from church that morning. I noticed they had an evening service, I loaded up my kids as fast as I could and off to church we went.

When I walked in the church door the same kind man, Ted, walked up to me; he remembered my name. He asked, "Are these your kids, Luauna?"

When I answered, "Yes", he asked if I wanted to place them in children's church. I said, "No, thanks."

I didn't trust anyone to watch my kids. He just smiled and helped me find three seats. Again, this whole church thing was new to me. A few people came up to me and said hello. I'd never met so many nice people; they *must* be faking it! "Are they really sweet?" I thought to myself; their sweetness even made me a little nervous.

I followed everyone's lead again, standing up with them, and sitting down when they did. Something again was happening inside my heart. I felt like crying again, but this time I just took a deep breath and swallowed down the lump in my throat. I felt a presence again; every hair on my arms was standing up. Each service was easier and easier, and I loved God's presence.

I loved to watch the people sing; little by little I was learning the songs. I especially liked to watch the man who stood up in front, shining with God's love. He was short and barely could look over the pulpit, but he would just smile as he sang. No, he wasn't the best singer, but he sure loved Jesus. One day, he walked up to me, reached out his hand to shake mine and said, "My name is Henry. Glad you are coming to church, you keep coming, and you'll get stronger and stronger." Then he smiled, turned and walked away.

I was *determined* to "get stronger and stronger", as Henry promised. After about a week, I felt something happening. I was feeling troubled inside. I was reading my Bible every day, but my body was going through cocaine withdrawals, and I felt darkness all around me. I couldn't sleep at night, and was becoming paranoid for some reason. I had never felt such fear. I didn't tell anyone at church, because I didn't know anyone.

Going on the second week, I wasn't sure that I was going to make it. One young lady would always smile at me from across the church. She walked up to me and said "Hello", handed me her phone number, and said if I ever needed anything, to please call her. I was very much a loner, and just smiled.

Then she said, "Hang in there, you'll make it." She asked for my phone number. I had never given my phone number away to anyone, but for some reason I gave it to her.

After service I went home and tried to sleep; again darkness surrounded me. Fear rose up; in the middle of the night as I was finally dozing off, I would hear strange noises. I had never noticed those noises before; I'd lived by myself for a long time, my two kids and I. Where were these strange feelings coming from? Not sleeping for days had its toll on me. Then after a midweek evening service the same young lady walked up and asked me, "Luauna, how are you doing? Are you OK?"

I had never opened up to anyone, but I found myself telling her what was happening.

She said, in her soft, gentle voice, "The devil's mad at you. He's just tormenting you."

I replied, "Yeah, he's doing a good job; I'm not sure I'm going to make it."

The service was over, I turned and walked out. I put my kids down to sleep, and started to read my Bible. Again, this overwhelming darkness surrounded me. I felt so much fear, I couldn't sleep. Then all of a sudden my phone rang; it was late and I wondered, "Who's calling me at this hour?"

I answered the phone; it was the young woman from church. She said, "Luauna, I could not stop thinking about you, I want to pray for you. Is it OK if I come over?"

She was at my house in about twenty minutes. She looked at me and said, "Luauna, I can tell you're struggling. Come on, you need to get some sleep. How many nights have you not slept?" I told her a few. I shared with her how I did cocaine every day before I got saved. I said, "I'm not sure if what I'm feeling is withdrawals. I feel such darkness. I'm even hearing voices telling me to do a line of cocaine and I would be fine."

She looked at me and said, "IT IS SATAN. He's trying to pull you back into the world. Come on, I'm going to stay with you while you get some sleep."

I walked into my bedroom, and she followed me. I turned around and my defense went up immediately. She could tell I didn't trust her. She reached for a chair and placed it beside my bed, and said, "Please get some sleep." I lay down and she reached over and placed her hand on my shoulder and started praying. I heard her as she was asking the Holy Spirit to keep watch over me.

I must have fallen right to sleep. I slept hard; when I woke up I was surprised to see her still sitting in the same chair. She smiled, and said, "OK, I'm going home now." Then she turned around and said, "Ask God to fill you with His Holy Spirit Power." I looked at her; she continued, "When you read your Bible look up Holy Spirit."

I was like a sponge; when she told me to look up the Holy Spirit, that's just what I did. I took a marker, and every time I saw the words "Holy Spirit," or "Holy Ghost," I highlighted them. I was so new, and needed something to help me make it.

For a few days this young lady came to my house every night. She was like an angel. She shared her story with me, how she had been raped as a little girl, had become a prostitute, and how she hated herself. Then one day someone told her about Jesus, and how Jesus changed her whole life. I was shocked how she opened up to tell me about her life. She shined God's light, and I needed that light during this terrible time of darkness.

Time passed and I was filled with the Holy Spirit. Wow, talk about a change! It seemed strange; I had a whole new strength and power from above. I still had battles for the first three months of my new walk in Jesus. It seemed like every day brought new changes.

❧❧❧❧❧❧❧❧❧❧❧❧❧❧❧❧❧❧❧❧❧❧❧❧❧❧❧❧❧❧

I'd wanted to be an attorney before I was saved, and had started attending college. Since I was a single mother with two children, it was hard to work and go to school at the same time, but I did. I had just finished a class where we were told to go sit in the courtroom, listen and take notes, and then write a report. After sitting through the court case I was so angry- the rapist got away! He had more money and obviously a better attorney. When I came back to class, I threw down my books, exclaimed, "There is no justice!" and walked out.

When I began my law studies, I also put myself through Barber College, because I could make better money doing hair than waitressing.

I loved hair styling; it became an outlet for the artist in me. Before long I was wrapped up in the beauty field, and after graduating I had a following of clients. I had also started competing in hair competitions, which gave me the experience and ability to make even more money. I took second place for the state of Colorado. I headed for the National Competition, which was held in St. Louis, Missouri that year, and finished second place. After that, I was preparing for the World Competition in Japan, but God had another plan. All of this was before I became a Christian. The beauty field was a good moneymaking profession, but it was also saturated with hidden drugs. I was very shy and the only way I could be up on stage for a hair show was when I was high on cocaine. Noticing my shyness, someone had introduced me to cocaine, and it became my drug of choice. The only thing I didn't know was it was becoming an invisible prison, A DEATH TRAP!

After I became a Christian, I realized I used cocaine because I was covering all the pain of my past. I was hiding behind a deadly enemy, and it was just waiting for the perfect time to kill me. I was making really good money, and was cutting the hair of the main cocaine dealers; they loved the job I did, they made sure I had plenty of cocaine. The devil's trap indeed!

After I came to Jesus, I realized the need to quit my job. The place I worked was not good for me, because every time I turned around someone was offering me cocaine. One day, I packed all my stuff and walked out. I had put enough money away to hold me over for about one year. I owned a few mobile homes and I knew I needed to sell those as well. There were too many people from my past. I rented a little, tiny cottage not far from the church, downsized and moved out. Thank GOD I did; later my mobile home was riddled with bullets, and a young woman was found dead in the trash dumpster outside my old home.

For one year, all I did was read my Bible all day long, go to church and I LOVED every bit of it. My kids and I were so much happier now. I really didn't know how to raise them, I went to the Christian bookstore, bought all of Dr. James Dobson's books and started reading those along with my Bible. Boy, did I have a lot of changing to do.

The first year I must have wept during every church service. I'd found something real, for the first time in my life. My heart was healing little by little. I was still closed off to the people, no one really knew much about me, and I was still very insecure. But I was discovering that I was created for God's purpose. I had been rejected my whole life it was hard to really believe that God knew me and loved me.

WHERE CAN I GO?

3

Psalm 116:1-4 "I love the Lord, because He has heard my voice and my supplications. Because He has inclined His ear to me, therefore I will call upon Him as long as I live. The pains of death encompassed me, and the pangs of Sheol laid hold of me; I found trouble and sorrow. Then I called upon the name of the Lord: 'O Lord, I implore You, deliver my soul!'"

I felt so happy inside this my new life in Jesus. It didn't even matter that I lived in a tiny matchbox house with my son and daughter. We were as happy as could be, and nothing else was important. I read the Bible in comic form every day to my kids. When they were lying down to sleep I read it again. I made highlights in my Bible with a yellow marker, and read Dr. Dobson's books before I went to sleep.

No one knew my background, and I wasn't about to share it with anyone because when I looked around at church everyone looked so sweet and kind. I was embarrassed to tell anyone I had come from a broken home.

Talk about *dysfunctional*- we were it...

My mother had been married and divorced eight times, not including all the boyfriends in between. She was like a man magnet; everywhere she went, heads turned her way. Her beauty was her downfall. She was very beautiful: almond-shaped brown eyes, coal black hair, and ruby red lips. Every hair was always in place, and she was the picture of sheer style in every stitch of clothes she wore. Her figure was a perfect, 36-26-36; with her three-inch spiked high heel shoes, and tight miniskirts she looked like she was right out of a movie.

She may have looked fantastic, but I hated my mother's life style. I share more about that part of our life in my other book, "A Mother's Story," I don't want to repeat myself in this book, but I need to share some of my past.

When I was a little girl around 4 years old my mother decided she didn't want kids. She dressed me up in a white collared blouse, pleated navy skirt, white ankle socks and black patent leather shoes. We walked to the car and I sat in the back seat. My feet barely dangled over the edge of the seat but I sat quietly. I remember looking at my mother through the rearview mirror; she reminded me of a movie star. That day as I sat in the car I didn't know that my mother was taking me to a place called Sacred Heart Orphanage, in Pueblo, Colorado. We drove up to the massive brick building with a big black wrought-iron fence that surrounded the grounds. My mother took my hand as I got out of the car and in her other hand she had a suitcase. As we walked through the big gate, two nuns walked towards us. Of course when I was young I didn't know what these strange ladies were who dressed so weird. One lady was dressed in all white from the top of her head to the bottom of her feet, and the other all in black. They wore those long dresses, and their heads and necks were covered. I was scared, and hid behind my mother, but she pulled me out from behind her. One nun reached out her hand and asked me if I wanted a banana, and if I wanted to walk with her to the swings. I said a quick "NO Thank you!"

My mother told me, "Luauna, go with this nice lady," and she put my hand in hers. I remember walking towards the swings and I kept looking towards my mother. This strange lady kept asking me questions, but I didn't want to talk to her. I wanted my mother. Then all of a sudden my mother turned around and walked towards the big iron gate. As she walked out it closed and locked. I jumped up and ran across the grass after her, but when I got to the gate it didn't open. I tried to open it, pushing it frantically, pulling and shoving it forward, yelling as loud as I could as my mother got into her car and drove away. "DON'T LEAVE ME MOM, DON'T LEAVE ME!" I tried to open the gate but couldn't. I pushed the gate as hard as I could, then I held on to the bars with both hands just looking between the bars as my mother drove down the street and around the corner. I just stood there weeping for what seemed to be forever, repeating my cry, "Don't leave me, please don't leave me," but she was gone.

The nun in the white dress came and stood beside me, as I stood holding on to the gate with both hands. She went to reach for one of my hands but I pulled away: "Where's my mom?"

She squatted down and said, "Luauna, it's going to be OK." She reached for my hand again; again I pulled it away. She said, "Come on, let me show you around."

Rejection is a terrible thing to feel as a child. Feeling unwanted and unloved is such a demon force that takes hold of a vulnerable heart, and its grip can be overwhelming. I spent a few years in the orphanage.

By the time I was fifteen years old, I was released from a place called CYC, Colorado Youth Center. When I finally went home my mother was in between husbands. I went to school, and worked at a small Mexican restaurant as a dishwasher at night, in order to pay for my school clothes, and buy the things I needed for school. I did my best to stay clear of my mother; I didn't want to bother her, but during the weekends I needed a ride home after work. I worked some shifts until closing, 12 midnight and others until 1:30 a.m. It was all right at first because my mother went out dancing and when the club would close she would come pick me up afterwards. I sometimes had to wait outside for her. I would hide in the alley because she wouldn't pick me up until 2:30 or 3:00 a.m. I always knew when she met a new boyfriend, but I didn't care because then she would be much happier.

My two younger sisters lived with their father; and my older sister was already married. My father left when I was born, I really never knew him as a young girl. My mother was starting to get impatient with me, although I had only been home a few months. At times she would forget to pick me up from work altogether.

One of those nights, I waited outside and huddled up next to the dumpster because it was so late and dark. I didn't want anyone to see me and try to pick me up. Earlier before closing a man came and sat at one of the tables. I gathered dishes, and bused tables. When I saw him, he was staring at me up and down. YUCK! I felt really uncomfortable.

He said, "It's almost closing time. Do you need a ride home?"

I answered, "No thanks, my mother's coming for me."

He just smiled with his strange crooked smile and kept staring. My mother knew this man and she would tell me, "He's such a nice boy, you should date him." No thanks! That night I couldn't wait until he left the restaurant. I called the bar and paged my mom to remind her, "Please don't forget to pick me up". But they put me on hold and then hung up.

I was hoping he would leave, and finally he did. Whew! I finished all my work and waited inside until the owner was ready to leave. My mother forgot me again. I was embarrassed to tell the owner, I just smiled and said, "My mom's coming for me any minute."

He said, "Ok." We walked outside together; he went to his car and drove off. I walked to the side of the building again, and hid by the dumpster. I thought about walking home but I was scared. After a while, I heard a car drive up very slowly. As I looked up it was the man my mother knew. I tried to hide and blend into the dark but he saw me. He said, "Luauna, I know you're there. Come on, I'll give you a ride home."

I wanted to just die! I stood up boldly, and said, "No thanks, my mother's coming for me any minute."

He knew my mother, smiled and said, "You know she's at the dance, you can't stay out here all night long."

"No thanks!"

He drove off again, and I wanted to run home, but we lived too far away. I hid again; it was getting later and later, and *no mom*. It was about 2:30 a.m. and I was tired, when all of a sudden he drove up again. He acted like he really cared. He leaned over and opened the front passenger door and said, "Come on now, I can't allow you to stay out here all night waiting for your mother, get in the car. I'll give you a ride home."

I just stood there. What was I going to do, should I get in the car or not? He looked around, and when he noticed I was nervous, said, "It's getting late! I'll give you a ride home." He made small talk, and I answered with yes and no answers.

He was driving right in the direction of my house, and I felt so relieved. When he turned and drove towards the front of my house, he started to slow down as if to stop. I reached to open the door handle, but suddenly I felt his whole arm reach around my head. He grabbed a hold of my hair tightly, pulled me right back into the car against him, and stepped on the gas. He had a tight grip on me. I tried to pull his arm from around my neck, but he had me in a head lock. He drove recklessly and jumped a curb and was driving now towards a school field. He was going behind the school yard. My heart was beating 90 miles an hour. He finally stopped, still holding me by a full hand of my hair. He turned me towards him. I saw an evil over this man; he just smiled at me and said, "I've been watching you for a while now."

I was scared and very angry. He reached under his seat and pulled out a hand gun. He pointed it right at my head, and told me how he wanted me. He reached to touch me, and I doubled up my fist and hit him as hard as I could. I yelled at him and told him, "You'll have to kill me before I let you touch me!"

Right after I said those words he doubled up his fist and hit me with a full blow to my face. He was hitting me, and I was hitting him right back as hard as I could. I fought for my life that night. I had never been with a man, and I wasn't about to let this man touch me. He hit me over and over; the gun must have fallen on the floor, because he was now hitting me with both hands. I don't know how it happened, but I must have hit the door handle and in the middle of fighting I fell out of the car to the ground. Don't ask me how I did it, but somehow I jumped to my feet and ran. I heard his car start up and he was coming after me. I ran between the houses, and jumped one fence after another until I got to my door. Only by God's grace, I reached for the house key still in my pocket, opened the door, turned around and locked it, and ran upstairs. My mother still wasn't home; I didn't turn on any lights. I ran upstairs to her bedroom, reached for the phone and pulled it under the bed with me to hide. I didn't know who to call! I was so frightened, and shaking, and then all of a sudden I heard a car drive up. Fear *gripped* my heart! I heard a car stop and the engine shut off; I hoped it was my mom, but I was too scared to get out from underneath the bed and look out the window. Then I heard a knock on the door, and his voice! He kept saying, "Luauna, I'm sorry. I didn't mean to hurt you. Open up the door, I'm sorry! Are you in there?"

I about died! Was he going to break into the house? I felt like my heart was beating so loud that the whole neighborhood could hear it. I sure could. I don't know why I was afraid to call the police. I cried and stayed hidden under the bed. He didn't break into the house, thank God, and after a while I fell asleep under the bed. I woke up early. I needed the bathroom. When I went to the bathroom, I was shocked when I looked up and saw my face. My lip was busted open; blood was all over my face and clothes from my nose bleeding. My eye was swollen and my whole face was bruised. Starting to cry, I washed off my face and got cleaned up.

Later my mother walked in, looked at me, and asked, "What happened to you?"

I told her, "Your friend, the nice guy, Alex, did this."

Mom just looked at me and asked, "What did you do to promote it?"

I answered in shock, "What! I didn't do anything, I did nothing!"

Turning around her parting word was, "I need to get ready for work."

Nothing more was said of that night. I was very hurt and angry I felt like a time bomb. I bought a dagger knife and kept it right in the side of my boot. This overwhelming rejection and worthlessness was *taking me captive*-and I was only fifteen years old.

I continued my routine of school during the day, then to work, still trying to stay out of my mother's hair. She was between boyfriends, and was not a happy camper. She'd told me once, after I'd come home from school, "I don't know why I had you kids! You're worthless and good for nothing." She'd always made that very clear. One day she told me, "Call your probation officer. You're going back to CYC. I don't want kids."

I remember asking her then, "Why did you have me? I didn't ask to come into this world! I'm not going back to CYC, it's unfair!" I just stood frozen because I knew she meant it.

The last time this "solution" occurred to her, I ended up in Zebulon Pike Detention Center, when I was only 12 years old. Mom's husband at that time beat me so bad I passed out; I thought he was going to kill me because I was 5 minutes late coming home from school. I ran away in the middle of the night after his last beating. That was when I was caught and placed In Zebulon Pike.

꧁꧂꧁꧂꧁꧂꧁꧂꧁꧂꧁꧂꧁꧂꧁꧂꧁꧂꧁꧂꧁꧂꧁꧂꧁꧂꧁꧂꧁꧂

My room had a steel bed, toilet, and sink- all gray; the walls were cinder brick painted cream white. The cold feeling of that heavy door closing behind you when it locked. It echoed through the room, it was a real eye opener and a wakeup call that I was now locked up. The small window had bars over it but you could barely see out. I counted every brick in the room, and every tile on the floor, I found myself trying to make out people's names etched into the walls under the paint. The itchy gray blanket with white dingy sheets and small pillow were really not comfortable.

It was not long before I got into one fight after another. I was so angry inside; a bitter seed of poison was growing deep within.

The doors would open for shower time once daily. I was insecure, and I hated for anyone to look at me. I was shy, I tried to hurry in and hurry out. One day, five of us girls were told to hurry in and take our showers. I went in first, hurried up and wrapped a towel around me to walk out, but I was met by three girls. One was the bully of the place; she started making fun of me. She acted like she was a boy, and I knew what she was trying to do. She reached for my towel, and I took a step back and hit her hand away. She motioned for the other girls to surround me. I remember my jaw tightening up, and I thought to myself, "I'd better jump first or they are all going to get the best of me."

The bully stepped forward towards me to grab my towel again, but instead of waiting for her to hit me I tackled her like a football player. What I didn't know was I caught her off guard; she slipped on a bar of soap and fell back, hitting her head on the hard tile wall and then the floor. Her head cracked open and blood was everywhere. I was already in a rage, as she went down I jumped on her and kept hitting her while her friends were hitting me. I pounded her head down over and over again, against the floor, not realizing there was blood on the floor. My hair was long to my waist, I didn't know my nose was bleeding as well. I couldn't see anything through my hair; the scratches her friends gave me were also bleeding. I stayed sitting on top of her, hitting her until the guards came flying in and broke it up. Everyone said I started it, but I didn't care anymore.

I said nothing. I was placed in solitary confinement for what seemed like forever. They brought me old smelly bologna sandwiches with what seemed like stale bread with mustard every day for lunch. Today YUCK, I can't stand the smell of bologna. I closed off more and more. I hated myself, and wondered why I was even born.

Being in a detention center only fueled my anger and rejection. I hated myself and everyone else, and felt like I couldn't trust anyone in my life.

What I thought was going to be a few weeks in Zeb Pike ended up being more time than I could remember. I was filled with so much anger by now, and it wasn't hard to find a reason to fight inside this facility. I was a loner, just sitting on a table beside the window looking out every day, thinking of ways to run away. I remember a counselor, who was also a guard; his name was Jerry. He tried encouraging me to join all the other kids playing different games, but I was insecure and filled with hate, I would just look at him, then turn around and stare out the window. One day he dismissed all the kids back to their rooms. He said, "Everyone except you, Luauna."

I stayed sitting on top of the table, I didn't move and I didn't care why he told me to stay back. After everyone went back to their rooms, Jerry walked into his office and came back out with a basketball. He walked beside the table and gently rolled the ball to me. I looked at him with a stiff jaw, and turned my head and looked outside. He tried a few times, but I gave him no response.

Then he walked back into his office and came out with two pairs of boxing gloves. He walked up to the table again, only this time he threw a pair at me and told me to put them on. I glanced at the gloves, then looked at him, and turned my head back towards the window. Again he told me, "Luauna! Put those boxing gloves on now." It was a stare down; I just looked at him.

Again, he said, "Right now, get them on!"

By this time I was mad, I reached over and grabbed the boxing gloves, looked at him, cursed and yelled, "WHAT! You like hitting women? Whatever!"

I cursed, and put my hands in the gloves, and just stood there. Then he walked right in front of me. He took little jabs, one after another, not hard, but egging me on. Until, all of a sudden, I was furious I went right after him hitting him with everything I had; over and over I was hitting him. Then all of a sudden he grabbed me, put his arms around me and held me as I was fuming inside.

As he held me with both arms wrapped around me and said, 'Little one, I don't why, or who made you so angry. But you've got to get it all out because if you don't it's going to destroy you."

I stood there shaking, filled with anger. I threw the gloves on the floor and he told me, "Ok, you can go to your room." I tried to run away from that place but got caught and was locked in solitary confinement.

❧❧❧❧❧❧❧❧❧❧❧❧❧❧❧❧❧❧❧❧❧❧❧❧❧❧❧❧

When Christmas time came, for me it was like any other day. I remember my mother and stepfather came to visit me at Christmas. I was called to the visitor's room along with other kids. I sat down in the visitor's room and thought, "Why is my mother with this man here, visiting me, pretending like they care?"

I sat with my arms crossed; I couldn't care less if they came to see me or not. The only reason I was in Zeb Pike was because I ran away to protect myself from his beatings. As I sat in the chair, they sat right across from me with a small coffee table between us. They opened up a bag, my stepfather pulled out a Christmas present and started to lean over the little table to hand it to me. Our eyes locked, and I pushed the present right back at him and said, "I don't want one thing from YOU."

As I was leaning to push the present back to him he stood up, and I stood up too. He looked at me and I glared right back at him. He drew back his hand and hit me right in the face.

Before I knew what happened he went to hit me again; only this time the counselor, Jerry, the same man who made me put on the boxing gloves, flew out of his office. He jumped over the little table, grabbed my stepfather by the collar, and shoved him up against the wall. He yelled to the main office, "Ring the buzzer!"

You couldn't open the door without someone ringing and releasing the lock, it was a double security door. As the buzzer rang, Jerry was yelling, "No wonder that little one is filled with hate. You want to fight, hit a man!" He threw my stepfather out both doors and stood at the door. I think he was waiting for my stepfather to step up and fight. By this time, my mother was already out the door.

I stood watching this whole thing happen. When Jerry came back in he was pretty riled up. He came right to me and said, "Let me see your face, are you ok?"

I looked at him. I was shocked. He patted my head, smiled, and said, "We showed him, didn't we. Ok, go to your room and get some rest, dinner is almost ready."

I went to my room that afternoon and lay on my bed. I couldn't believe this; the last time I ever remembered someone standing up for me was just before my mother placed me in an orphanage. My grandpa stood in front of my mother and yelled, "Why don't you leave her with me? Don't put her in that place." At the time I had no idea it was me my grandfather was asking for. No one else had ever stood up for me.

I felt confused; I pushed all those thoughts way back in my heart and mind. Thinking, "You can't trust anyone anyway." Jerry and I went on as if nothing had happened that day.

✤✜✤✜✤✜✤✜✤✜✤✜✤✜✤✜✤✜✤✜✤✜✤✜✤✜✤✜✤✜✤✜✤✜✤✜✤

A few months later, I had a court date; my mother and stepfather were in the courtroom, sitting with a woman who didn't look very friendly. Everyone talked back and forth, and then all of a sudden my stepfather stood up and said, "Your honor, this child is in need of supervision. She is a delinquent." I didn't know what that word meant, but it sure sounded bad. After a few more questions the judge said, "Ok, I'm placing Luauna in Morrison Detention Center, in Denver, Colorado." He said a few other words I didn't understand, and- just like that! - the judge rose from his chair and walked through the door behind him.

I didn't know what was happening; I was about to turn 13 years old at the time. Looking around, I glanced towards my mother. She slightly smiled, then looked down, and then I noticed two sheriff deputies walking towards me. One stood on my right and another on my left. I looked towards my mother and said, "What's going on? Where am I going?" They ordered me, "Luauna, please stand up!"

As I stood up, they asked for my hands and placed handcuffs on me. They went on, "Let's go."

I asked, "Where?" I looked at my mother; I didn't understand what had happened. I was led out a side door and a police car was waiting for me. I looked out the back window of the police car as we drove away and saw my mother and stepfather watching.

"Where am I going?" I asked the policeman who was driving, "Where are you taking me?"

He said, "To Morrison Detention Center. It's in Denver, Colorado."

I asked, "Why?" He looked at me through the mirror and said nothing. I sat back in the seat that day, and felt deep hatred inside. I was seething with feelings of hurt and rejection that day.

The drive from Colorado Springs to Denver seemed like it took forever. Finally, we drove up to a great big gate. I looked around and said, "This looks like a prison."

Little did I know, that's exactly what it was; only this place was for young kids who were considered delinquent. It was stricter than Zebulon Pike Detention Center. As we drove in and noticed people walking around, I wondered if they were girls who were locked up, and thought they looked older than I was. Later, I found out almost everyone was older than I was.

The policeman checked me in, and gave my file to the person at registration. Then he turned, walked out, and drove off; those big gates closed right behind him. I was asked if I had anything and told to empty all my pockets. I was given a list of rules and told to follow the staff over to hospital cottage. Everyone who comes in has to stay in hospital cottage for a few days. I didn't say a word, just followed them. I was scared to death, but wasn't about to let anyone know what I was really feeling.

Hospital cottage was far from a cottage! It was an infirmary in a woman's prison lock down. I was told, "Strip, all clothes off."

I was so shy; I stood there, and asked the lady if she had something I could put on. She didn't smile one bit, looked at me right in the eye and said, "I said, strip your clothes off, all of them." She looked at me as I just stood there. Then she said, "If we have to take your clothes off its not going to be very fun for you. But if that's what you want, that's what we'll do."

I felt my anger rise up inside. Then I turned and took off my clothes. She led me to a bathtub, and told me to sit inside of it. It didn't have any warm water; it was porcelain and cold as I sat naked in that empty tub. She called another woman in who had in her hand a small packet of white powder. She said, "Keep your eyes closed."

She poured the powder all through my hair. At that time it was long, almost to my waist. She told me, "Rub it through all your hair." I had to sit with this gross smelling white powder all over my head and body.

After a little while she walked back in with a bottle of white liquid and poured it over my head, and said, "Make sure this gets all over your body." The white powder with the white liquid was *disgusting*. I felt like I was going to throw up. I was made to sit in this paste of a dreadfully smelling substance. Later, I learned everyone who came into Morrison had to be disinfected, in case anyone had lice.

I made it through the first few days I was in lockdown, until I was finished going through all of their required tests. While I looked outside through my window, I noticed a few "men" cleaning up the grounds. Later, I discovered they were neither boys nor men; they were girls acting like boys and men. What I didn't know was these same girls acting like boys had their eye on me, and before I was even out of hospital cottage they were already laying claim to me.

I was one of the youngest and let me tell you, I learned how to fight at the drop of a hat. Some of these girls would try to push their lifestyle on the girls who walked in fear. They would bully them until they gave in to them. It was so sad to watch. But I was already like a time bomb. I was angry, it didn't take much to trigger me into a fight, and I didn't even care if a fight cost me time in solitary confinement. After a while I felt more protected in confinement, or restricted to my room; I didn't care one way or the other.

One week went by and I was finally given a uniform and taken to a new dorm like a cellblock. As I walked in, it looked like a big cottage. But as you entered there was a desk in a lockdown office. Double security lockdown doors were in place. It had two floors; the main room was set up like a big front room, with tables, chairs, couches, and bookshelves. I could look up and see all the doors on the upper floor and doors on the lower floor, about 40 rooms total.

No one was in the building at the time I was being checked in. They walked me up to my room on the upper floor and gave me a list of rules. They turned around and walked out of my room. The door slammed closed and it locked. The only way it opened was if someone rang the buzzer or someone had a key. I felt all alone. Looking around this small room, I saw a toilet in the corner and small metal sink, barred windows, and a desk was built right into the wall up against the window. I jumped up and sat with my back to the wall, my feet up on top of the desk so I could look outside the window. I wondered as I sat on top of that desk, "Why was I born? Why did my mother hate me so much? Why did my father leave? Maybe- if he would have met me-*maybe* he might have liked me."

Being in Morrison was a whole new ballpark; the girls in this place were just as angry as I was. It wasn't long before someone started a fight with me. I found myself fighting all the time to protect myself. I was angry and I didn't care. I was small and skinny but I was a tomboy. I had run track and field and was strong. One fight led right into another, and before long I was locked in solitary confinement. A small padded room, with only a toilet and metal sink. When I say padded, I mean the whole place was padded; I slept on the floor with only my underwear, because they'd taken my clothes. It was their way of breaking you down. I counted every padded square in that room, from the floor to the ceiling.

It seemed like I was always in trouble, constantly fighting. It was like I lost control. Anything anyone would say would set me off. I got the nickname, "Bullet." After the first years of fighting, people started leaving me alone. I was closing off more and more. I always told myself I was ugly, fat and stupid. Those words were ringing in my head over and over, after all my mother said I was worthless.

After a few years, I was released into another program. This program was the one before you are released from juvenile confinement and sent home. The time came and I was told that I would be going into CYC (Colorado Youth Center). I was going to turn 15 in a few months. I knew if I did well it wouldn't be long before I would be sent back home. It went like clockwork: I did well, a court date was set, and I would be released to go home. My mother came to the court; she wasn't married anymore. She gave the impression that she wanted me home. The judge gave me the date I was to be released. I was packed and ready; a bit scared, but I wanted out.

෴෴෴෴෴෴෴෴෴෴෴෴෴෴෴෴෴෴෴෴෴෴෴෴෴

This is why I took a job in the little Mexican Restaurant to help pay for the things I needed for school, and help out with whatever was needed around the house. When my mother told me to call my probation officer, she wanted me to go back to CYC, I knew she meant it. I had only been home for about 6 months. Even though I tried to stay out of her way, she was always angry, screaming and threatening to send me back.

At work there was a guy who didn't live too far from me. When he found out that I was waiting outside for my mother, he told me where he lived and he could give me a ride to and from work. I knew him and I didn't feel that "yucky" feeling like the other guy. He started giving me a ride home. I thought it would make my mother happy since she didn't have to give me a ride to work or pick me up. But nothing changed; she kept yelling at me the minute I got home from school. Every day it was getting more and more heated between my mother and me.

When he picked me up, the gentleman, Sam would honk the horn. I'd run outside with my bag in hand so he didn't hear all the fighting. One day, I didn't hear him honk, he made it all the way to the door. My mother was screaming so loud I didn't hear him ring the doorbell. All of a sudden I heard his loud knock; I looked at the clock and knew it was Sam. I ran, bolted through the door and closed it fast behind me. He looked at me as I ran to the car. I was beet red from embarrassment; I knew he'd heard us fighting from the door. I sat quietly in the car, and half way to work he asked, "What's going on with you and your mom?"

My face flushed red and I yelled, "Why don't you mind your own business?"

He didn't say much after that, but before work he said, "I can solve your problem for you."

I looked at him and said, "Yeah right."

"Sure, you can marry me."

I looked at him like, "SICK! No thanks!"

A few weeks went by; things grew worse between my mom and me. She wanted me out, and truth be told I wanted out as well. One day, I realized my mother was going to call and find out about placing me back in CYC. That day I went to work thinking, "What should I do?"

Then it hit me! I went over to talk to the guy who gave me rides to and from work and asked him, "Is your offer still open?"

He looked at me and said, "*What* offer?"

I reminded him, "You said you wanted to marry me; do you want to marry me or not?"

He was shocked, but I was more shocked, when he looked at me up and down and said, "Yes!" I didn't love this man; he was a good man, but I didn't love him.

I went home and told my mother, "I'm getting married."

She said, "Good!"

The date was set; when that day came, we all piled into the car and headed off to the courthouse in Colorado Springs. Here we were-the guy from work, my mother, and I. I stood in front of the judge. At 15 ½ years old, I felt my eyes fill with tears, thinking how much I did not want to get married. The judge looked at me and then asked, "Young lady, is someone making you get married?"

I was silent for a moment, and answered, "No, sir."

He looked at the paper work in front of him for a little while. Then the judge stopped again. He looked up and said, "I don't know what's wrong with this picture, but something *isn't* right. I can't marry you; this young lady is only 15 ½ years old. I can't do it. If I do this I won't be able to live with myself, and won't be able sleep tonight." He pushed the paperwork forward and shook his head, saying, "I'm sorry."

My mother was very upset, but I was happy, almost relieved. Then she reached for the papers and said, "Let's go."

I turned around and followed her out the door. She was cursing and talking under her breath all the way out of the courthouse. We drove down the street; all of a sudden my mother stopped in front of a print shop. She changed my birth date, and ran it through some type of copier. Then we all got back into the car, and off we drove to Pueblo, Colorado. My mother ordered me, "And when we get to the court house, don't cry! Do you understand?"

"Yes."

Later that afternoon I was a married woman. Really, I was a married little girl. I'd never been with a man. This is no way for anyone to get married! I was a broken little girl, and so lost inside. I didn't know how to love. This wasn't a love to build a marriage on; it was an escape. Did it get better? No, I only felt worse. I felt used, lonely and even more alone. It wasn't Sam's fault; he was only trying to fix a problem between my mother and me.

We hadn't been married very long, less than one year, when one day we went out with a group of friends. Everyone had been drinking, including the driver and his girlfriend in the front seat. We were heading up to the top of Pikes Peak. I didn't really want to go, but went anyway. There were four of us sitting in the back seat. When we reached the top, we stopped for a little bit, and then headed back down the mountain.

The driver by this time was angry with his girlfriend, and they started screaming and fighting as he drove down the mountain. Still under the influence, he turned and hit his girlfriend while driving. Then he started speeding down the hill. I was scared. I told Sam, "Please tell him to slow down, he's driving way too fast!"

I felt my whole body tense up. I placed one hand on the back of the driver's seat, as we were swerving around the curves, and braced both of my feet against the bottom of the back of the driver's seat. With my other hand I covered up my face. I yelled, "PLEASE STOP DRIVING FAST! TELL HIM TO SLOW DOWN," but he only went faster.

Then suddenly something broke and we went into a spin, around and around we went about three times, and then the car went right off a cliff. I think we might have rolled the car, it was so smashed. The only thing that kept us from rolling all the way down the hill was a tree that stopped us.

The driver flew right out the windshield, and landed by the tree; if it weren't for that tree we would have rolled right over him. The car was at an angle, the driver's door was open, and I could see the driver lying on the ground. He went into convulsions. The girl sitting next to him turned around and screamed; she was in shock. The whole side of her face was smashed: her cheekbone was broken and her eye looked as if it were hanging half out of the socket. She passed out. The girl sitting next to me had broken her back, and wouldn't be able to walk for a long time. Her boyfriend went into complete shock jumped out the side window and yelled, "Every man for himself!" He had been to Vietnam, and I think the wreck triggered something in his brain. He was trying to climb back up the top of the mountain, when someone tackled him and held him down. What no one knew was that a large piece of glass was lodged in his leg and blood was everywhere.

Sam was bruised and had some broken ribs; someone pulled him out of the back car window. They helped everyone out of the car, because they thought it was going to blow up. Smoke was everywhere-lots of dust and broken glass. They tried to pull me out of the back window, but the pain was so bad, and my legs were trapped in the back of the driver's seat. I yelled, "STOP!"

Someone had seen us go over the edge of the road, and they'd already called the police. When the ambulance arrived, the paramedics cut the car in order to get me out. I had broken hips, fractured pelvis, a cracked femur, and a dislocated right shoulder. We were all in a terrible mess! Everyone was hurt badly; three of us were taken to one hospital, and three to another. I spent several months at the hospital in traction, and it took about a year before I could walk.

Little by little my husband and I were growing apart. We were like two ships on a great big ocean. He was a hard worker, loved music, played the guitar, sang, and played drums. He also loved to dance and party. Sam was older than I was and we really had nothing in common.

I felt lost, and trapped. Without Jesus what does one have? Nothing! Not one thing!

But now I had something real. Salvation! When I think back how the devil tried over and over to kill me. I love Jesus more and more.

I'VE SEEN THEE FORSAKEN

4

Isaiah 54:6-8: "'For the Lord has called you like a woman forsaken and grieved in spirit, like a youthful wife when you were refused," says your God. "For a mere moment I have forsaken you, but with great mercies I will gather you. With a little wrath I hid My face from you for a moment; but with everlasting kindness I will have mercy on you,' says the Lord, your Redeemer."

Sharing my heart and life at times is still painful, but the reason I share is hope. *When you're in a situation that looks like there's no way out, believe me when I say, "Nothing is too hard for Jesus," I mean it. Allow me to go deeper to help you to know how God is able to bring someone up out of the Pit of Despair.*

After a few years of being married, I found out that I was going to have a baby. How was I going to take care of a baby? I was only a baby myself. I remember walking for miles and miles every day of my pregnancy. My belly was getting bigger and bigger. Then one night, about 11 p.m., a pain hit my body, and my water broke; it was time, and I was in full labor. All night long I was in hard labor and great pain. The doctor came into my room early in the morning and told me, "We'll need to take the baby out by caesarian; your baby's having trouble." I had broken my hips in the car accident, it was too hard for me to give birth naturally.

When I woke up, I learned I had a baby boy. We had picked out names for a boy or a girl; but- "It's a boy!"- so, we named him Samuel.

At that time I hadn't realized I had been out for a few days. I woke up in great pain. I remember asking them, "Where is my baby?" They brought my beautiful baby boy to me. Samuel was very cute, with a full head of hair, black as coal. I couldn't believe this little one came from me; I wanted to cry! He was little and fragile; so helpless. I opened up the blanket to see his little feet; I remember counting all his tiny toes, and he started kicking his legs back and forth, almost like he was telling me, "I'm cold, cover me up!" as his little fingers gripped my finger. His hand was so small!

I felt like I'd been run over by a Mack Truck. I didn't realize there could be so much suffering from having a baby. A few days went by, and my mother came to see me; she was acting strangely nice. My sister came to see me with her husband, who had been smoking pot and he was wired, "high as a kite." His eyes were all red from the marijuana, and he kept looking at me.

They stood right beside my bed, both of them red-eyed. I thought it was strange, their coming to see me; it wasn't like them to show concern. This was awkward; we all looked at each other. I was lying in bed, weak as ever. My sister's husband reached over and patted my forearm, looked me in the eye and said, "Wow, man! I'm really sorry about the cancer." Quickly my sister elbowed him and yelled, "Shut up, Stupid! You're not supposed to say anything!" He turned and said to my sister, "Oops, I forgot." Then they hurriedly said good-bye and left. My husband, Sam, would come to see me after work.

I was in too much pain to catch what they said right away. I was feeling sicker and sicker. Everyone was being too nice; it was not normal at all. All I wanted to do was hold my baby without pain. The doctor wouldn't allow me to nurse Samuel, telling me that the meds I was taking would affect the baby through breast milk.

Something strange was going on. I wasn't getting better; I was throwing up and felt increasingly weak. Later it hit me- the words my sister's husband said *finally* hit me! "CANCER," I thought to myself, "WHAT is going on?" Later that evening, when everyone came to see me again, the doctor walked in to see how I was doing. I think I shocked my family when I told them to get out of my room; I wanted to speak only to the doctor. After they all left the room, I looked the doctor right in the eye and asked, "You want to tell me what's going on? What's this thing about cancer?"

The doctor was shocked! I lifted my voice and said, "I'm old enough to get married, have a baby; now you need to tell *me* what's going on right now!" He said, "I'm sorry, your mother thought you might not be able to take the news." I was suddenly enraged, and exclaimed, "How would *she* know?" I looked at the doctor, and told him, "From this day on, I don't want anyone to know anything about me or my body. I want you to come to ME ONLY, do you understand?" He was very nice and said he was truly sorry.

"Now, tell me about this cancer!"

The doctor said, "It's very serious; you have ovarian cancer. We are going to start you on treatments, and we have already been giving you some of the medicine you need to get through the treatments." Thank God I was young! I really never knew much about cancer. But I did know one thing for sure; I was sick and my body felt very weak.

A few weeks went by, and I was still in the hospital not getting much better. One evening my mother walked into my room, and asked me how I was feeling. I half smiled and replied, "I'm fine." She called me "Honey", and then asked if I needed something to drink or an extra pillow. I knew right then that something was really wrong- *she never called me Honey!* **Never!**

After a little while she walked up to my bedside and said, "I've been thinking about you being sick, and what would happen if something happened to you."

I asked, "What are you talking about?"

"How would someone take care of the baby if you didn't get better?" Reaching into her bag, she pulled out a handful of papers and said, "You should sign these papers for me right there." She pointed to a line for my signature.

"What are these papers?" I reached out my hand to take them from her. She must have thought I was going to sign them. She reached a pen out to me to write with, and pointed to the line. Suddenly I realized they were insurance papers in case I died from cancer, a policy for over $250,000.

I felt like my head was about to explode! I looked at her with every bit of strength I had, and said in a low, deep and angry slow voice, "You'll not get rich off of my DEATH, and I'm not dying for you or anyone else." I reached over with my other hand, and ripped those papers into a thousand pieces.

She yelled, "I'm just trying to look out for you!"

My Mom walked out and nothing more was said. I was seething inside, confused, and frightened. I lay in my bed with tears rolling down the sides of my face, wondering if I was going to die. Then with the next breath, I fought those thoughts down, repeating, "I'm not going to die for you or anyone else." I kept saying, "I will live and not die."

I didn't realize that I was quoting the Word of God.

My body was not getting any stronger, and I felt extremely ill, either throwing up on one end, or going out the other. I hated the way I felt, and thought to myself, "I need to get out of this hospital or I'm going to die in this bed!" I got up one day, pulled the IV's out of my arms and told them, "I'm leaving." I put on my clothes and slowly walked down the hall to get my baby and make my exit out the door.

The nurses of course said, "We're sorry; you're not ready to leave."

I looked at them and said, "Yes, I am!"

They tried to stop me as I walked out the door, but I'd made up my mind; I was not going to stay another day in that bed.

꧁꧂꧁꧂꧁꧂꧁꧂꧁꧂꧁꧂꧁꧂꧁꧂꧁꧂꧁꧂꧁꧂꧁꧂꧁꧂

Of course I was sick for months on end, trying to get all those meds out of my system. I bought a juicer and started juicing. I didn't know how to be a mother; when my baby would cry I didn't know what to do. I would check to see if he was wet or needed food. I didn't know how to hold him in my arms, to comfort him. Samuel had colic, and I was still sick and weak. We were a pair; I tried to do everything to make him stop crying. Sometimes I could only lay him beside me and look at him. I'd find myself saying, "I don't know what you want!" We just looked at each other and both of us would cry ourselves to sleep.

꧁꧂꧁꧂꧁꧂꧁꧂꧁꧂꧁꧂꧁꧂꧁꧂꧁꧂꧁꧂꧁꧂꧁꧂꧁꧂

After a while, my husband was staying out later and later after work. I would make dinner; he'd call and tell me he was going out with the guys. This became his routine so I stopped trying to make dinner. I was hurt, rejected, and always felt ugly. I imagined the reason my husband wasn't coming home until late was because I was ugly, and that he didn't want me anymore than my mother or father did.

I was trying to be a woman, yet this little girl was crying inside, and now I was a mother, trying to keep my head straight for my son's sake. I heard rumors about my husband sleeping with other women; one woman I knew personally. I blamed myself at the time, because I figured that I didn't know how to love.

I had a baby, and I continued to feel more alone than before. Our marriage was falling apart completely, crumbling before my eyes. We didn't talk; nothing much was said between us. We pretended all was well. I started getting phone calls from other women. That was before cell phones existed; you only had a landline phone.

When I answered the phone, "*She*" would ask for Sam. *She* would actually ask, "Who is this?" to which I'd sarcastically reply, "His wife!" Of course she'd hang up; after a while I didn't care. I was as cold as ice towards him when he came home. We were two people living under the same roof, never really knowing each other.

Without Jesus, you have neither comfort nor peace. I felt like a prisoner in my own home, I taught myself how to drive. Little by little I learned how to drive to the store.

When Samuel was two years old, I'd put him in a car seat and we'd head for the store, or to the gas station. That was my big adventure for the day. One day the gas cap was stuck, and I couldn't take it off. A man drove up in his clean, shiny "slick" mobile. He noticed I was having trouble. He jumped out of the car, and said, "Let me help you with that, young lady." Then, as he reached for the gas pump he asked me, "How much gas are you putting in your car?" He looked me right in the eye, and said, "What kind of man allows his beautiful wife to fill up her car? If you were my wife, I'd take good care of you."

I turned beet-red and said sarcastically, "YEAH, RIGHT! Well I'm not your wife, so excuse me," and I finished filling the tank. He smiled, went to his fancy car, and filled his gas tank.

I hurried and drove off, looking back through my rear view mirror; he too was looking my way as my car left the station. A few weeks passed, and the same man showed up at the gas station, and the same thing happened. He was nice and helped me again, while he tried to flirt with me. He made me nervous.

Weeks passed, and I grew tired of my husband not coming home until late at night. One day while he was at work, I went to the store, bought a *Cosmopolitan* magazine, some makeup, and then went home to learn how to put it on. I decided, "Enough is enough!" that day, "What's good for the goose is good for the gander."

By the time my husband came home from work, I was ready for a night out- new clothes, tight mini-skirt, makeup and my hair all done up. The minute he walked in, I was waiting by the door with the baby in hand. As Sam opened the door, he stopped and looked me up and down. He said, "WHOA!" I didn't wait for another word to be said; I handed Samuel over to him, and walked out the door. When he asked, "Where are you going?"

I yelled back what I'd just told myself, "What's good for the goose is good for the gander!" then got into the car and drove off.

I didn't know where I was going, had never been in a bar before, but I was going somewhere... I drove up and down the streets for a few hours, trying to figure out where to go. Then I passed a sign: "Dance and Bar, Happy Hour". (*YEAH, RIGHT! Don't believe that lie.*)

I thought, "I'm going into that place." I was scared to death, but tried not to show it. I walked into the bar; the music was low and the place was packed. This place had the lights down low, was filled with smoke, and smelled gross. The smell of beer to me had always smelled like pee- YUCK! I walked in and went over to one side close to the dance floor. I stood in the corner by a cigarette machine. I had never been in a bar, and watching the dance floor, I felt my hands tremble.

As I stood in that corner, someone walked up to me, stopped, and looked me right in the eye. He asked, "What are you doing in a place like this?"

I just stood frozen for a minute. Our eyes made contact; it was Joe- the man from the gas station who helped me with my gas cap! I half smiled and nervously asked, "What are you doing here?" I tried to turn away, and looked down at the dance floor.

He said, "You don't belong in a place like this. Come on; let's go have a cup of coffee someplace- how about Perkins?" Perkins was a nearby 24-hour restaurant, like Denny's. I started to feel really stupid and nervous. I think he knew it was my first time in a bar. I wanted to turn and run out the door, but couldn't. He said, "You don't have to worry. You can drive your own car and I'll drive mine."

I felt uncertain, but finally said, "Okay," and that I'd meet him there; I knew where it was. As I walked to my car, I felt a thousand butterflies in my tummy, but still drove on to Perkins. I parked and waited outside the restaurant for a little while. I could see his car on one side of the parking lot. I was scared, but pushed the fear down.

As I walked into the place, he met me, and already had a table for us. I sat across from him, not knowing what to say. He started talking and asking me why I was in the bar? He then asked, "Are you having trouble with your husband?" I just looked at him and said nothing. I was so insecure and shy, always thinking I was ugly, fat, and stupid.

Amazing how the devil can feed cruel and abusive words into your mind. What's even more amazing? I believed every word Satan whispered in my ear. I was only 120 pounds, yet I could see neither worth nor beauty in myself.

Joe kept the conversation going through the late evening. Soon it was after midnight. He saw me looking at the time, and said, "Come on now, please don't go!"

I was broken, hurting, and foolish. Sin destroys lives, and I was the target. I sat at that table, listening to him talk about everything and yet nothing. When the moment came to leave, I got up and he walked me outside to my car. He stopped and asked me to come to his house.

I looked at him with a blank stare, expressionless, thinking, "Do I want to go home?" but found myself thinking of all the different women who'd been calling my husband. I was feeding the rejection and fueling the hurt hidden deep within my heart. I told him, "Yes," and that night I went home with him.

⚜❧

The next day I felt filthy, filled with so much shame. I was overcome with guilt.

Two wrongs *do not* make anything right...EVER.

Covered with shame, and acting like nothing was wrong; I hated myself even more. The very thing I hated about my mother, I'd just done. When I closed my eyes, I tried to shut off what had happened, but it was like a movie, running through my head. I was tormented inside. Nothing changed in our marriage; we were growing further apart. Women called, and I got to a place where I would say, "This one sounds like a nice girl," and throw the phone in his lap. I found myself, again, walking and walking for miles every day, only this time I pushed a stroller.

Every night I felt shame; I couldn't wash it off.

One day while I was getting gas, Joe walked up to me again. He said, "I've been looking for you every day."

I glared at him, wanting to scream and cry at the same time. I looked him in the eye, and told him, "Leave me ALONE!"

*ᒍ*ᑐ*ᒍ*ᑐ*ᒍ*ᑐ*ᒍ*ᑐ*ᒍ*ᑐ*ᒍ*ᑐ*ᒍ*ᑐ*ᒍ*ᑐ*ᒍ*ᑐ*ᒍ*ᑐ*ᒍ*ᑐ*ᒍ*ᑐ*ᒍ*ᑐ*ᒍ*ᑐ*ᒍ*ᑐ*ᒍ*ᑐ*ᒍ*ᑐ*

A few months went by, and then one night I received a phone call. I was told that Sam had been drinking and was drunk in an alley. I knew something was wrong. The police were called, and he was in the alley, but he was found dead. The woman he was seeing was married; her husband came home, caught them together, and a fight broke out. The woman's husband had his friends with him, and they all had been drinking. It was an ugly scene. During the fight they ended up outside. Sam was hit on the back of the head with a crowbar. The blow to the head made him dizzy, he fell back, and hit his head on the curb. He was knocked out completely. When they realized he was unconscious, they panicked. They rolled down the driver's side window, picked my husband up, and placed him in the car headfirst, so that his head came down on the passenger's side floor. His feet were still sticking out of the driver's window. The blow to his head caused hemorrhaging, and it was not long before he choked on his own blood, and died that night.

"WHAT!" I was stunned, shocked, and numb all at the same time. My mind and thoughts were going around in circles, a thousand miles a minute. "He's dead, your husband is DEAD!"

I didn't know what to feel. Hurt and rejection seemed to plague my life, after all this time, they were continually shoved down deep within my heart.

People would ask me, "What are you going to do?"

I'd think to myself when someone asked that question, "Like I really know what to do!" Here I was, a young mother with a 2-year-old baby, and they were asking me what I was going to do?

Funeral plans were made, and before I knew it, I was sitting in front of a coffin, staring at my husband. Little Samuel was sitting in my lap, trying to play patty-cake. He didn't know what was going on. His daddy was dead; he would never see his daddy again. Sam would never see him grow up, play ball...

I couldn't believe all this; one day my husband was with me talking, then off to work, and the next moment he was dead. After the funeral my mother asked me to go to her house for the night. She said, "It's better if you're not alone tonight." I was numb, I agreed.

That night I lay in bed in a room that had been her piano room: it had two doors, and a crystal chandelier hanging from the ceiling. She'd made it into a beautiful master/visitor bedroom. My little boy was sound asleep right beside me. I looked at him, my mind filled with so many questions. I was exhausted, and finally fell in to a dead sleep. All of a sudden in this dark strange room, I felt a hand rubbing my leg. It was pitch dark; I tried to focus my eyes, and thought I was dreaming. I dozed off again, and once again, I woke to someone touching my leg; I was frozen, petrified! This hand was moving its way up my thigh, and then I realized someone was in my room. *Fear* gripped my heart. Then, with everything I had, I jumped up and went for the light. As the light went on, my mother's husband was running out the other door. He was in his underwear; no shoes or shirt. It was almost three in the morning. I got up and locked one door, and put a chair in front of the other.

I could barely get back to sleep. The following morning, my mother had already started breakfast, and her husband was in the front room; Samuel was sitting there on the floor. I stood over the coffee pot thinking, "Do I tell my mother what happened last night? Would she believe me?" As I was pouring a cup of coffee, my anger grew until I was as mad as a hornet. Suddenly, I heard Samuel scream like I had never heard him scream before. I dropped my coffee cup and ran to him. His back was arched, and he was crying in pain as he lay on the floor. As I ran in, I yelled, "What happened?" My mother's husband yelled back, "I told him to leave the Kleenex box alone! I saw Kleenex on the floor, and someone said the baby was pulling out Kleenex one at a time, throwing it in the air, and laughing as they were floating back down." I reached over to pick my boy off the floor. He was still crying.

I pulled up his t-shirt, and sure enough he'd been hit very hard, open-handed on his little back, leaving a full handprint. By this time mom's husband was standing over the pot of coffee. I jumped up and ran into the kitchen, and shouted, "WHO gave you the right to hit my son?" He turned around and gave me his crooked, wicked smile, as if to say, "Too bad, so sad." This triggered a reaction! I reached down in my side boot, pulled out a dagger knife, and ran at him. He didn't have a shirt on, and I placed the knife right to the bottom of his belly, and pushed him up against the refrigerator. I had one hand up towards his throat and the other hand leaning and pushing the knife just enough into his belly to make him freeze. I screamed, "If I ever catch you touching my son, I'll kill you!" Then I continued, "If you ever come near me"-- as my mother walked in and saw what was happening, she screamed my name.

"LUAUNA! Put that knife down!"

Still holding the knife to his belly, and looking at him right in the eye, I yelled, "Ask your sick pervert husband what he was trying to do to me last night. Ask HIM, whose bed he tried to climb into, SICK PERVERT!" His lip tightened, and so did my knife. It was only God's grace that kept me from pushing the knife all the way into his belly. I then yelled again, "YOU SICK PERVERT! DON'T YOU EVER COME NEAR ME!" I turned, ran into the front room, grabbed my son and walked out the door.

I got into the car, and drove home, angry and hurt. "When will this junk ever stop?" I asked myself. Was this all life had to offer? I went home and sat on the couch for hours, looking at my son who was sitting right beside me. He didn't know what I meant when I asked myself, "What are we going to *do*?"

SNARES & TRAPS

5

Job 22:10-11: "therefore snares are all around you, and sudden fear troubles you, or darkness so that you cannot see; and an abundance of water covers you."

Fear gripped my heart, and I didn't know what I was going to do. How was I going to take care of myself? How was I going to pay the rent? I wanted to stay in bed and put the covers over my head, hoping that when I awoke this would all be a nightmare- but it wasn't. I knew the rent was paid for the month, we were all right for a few weeks. I had about a week of feeling sorry for myself, and walked around like a zombie. Then one day I looked at my son; he was so carefree! - not a worry, with his smiles and the sparkle in his eyes as he looked up at me. I thought to myself, "I've got to get up and do something, anything."

I went through all of our papers and found something from the bank; we had an account with a little bit of money, which would hold us over for a few months. After the first few weeks, I got a knock on the door. I opened it to see a man standing there, with papers in his hand. He was coming for furniture that had not been paid for. I was surprised and asked him, "What happened?" But he wasn't concerned, and said, "Ma'am,

I'm here to repossess the furniture that wasn't paid for." He handed me the papers, and I moved out of his way. He and the other men walked in and started to carry my bed, couch, chair, and a few other things out the door.

I was numb, all I could think was, "WHATEVER!"

♪❀

We had two cars, but the one my husband was found in was still parked outside my door. I didn't want to drive it; there was still blood on the floor. I placed an ad in the newspaper: "68 Chevelle Super Sport, 283 bored-out engine, red with black stripes down the hood and top of trunk, black vinyl top, FOR SALE $100."

It was a racing car for sure, and it wasn't long before someone answered the ad. A father with his son came to look at the car. The father asked, "What's wrong with the car?"

"Nothing," I answered; I wasn't thinking how much it was worth, nor was I thinking about needing more money later.

The father asked, "So, what's the pitch? This is a great car."

I looked him in the eye, and told him, "My husband was found *killed* in it; I want it out of here."

He opened his wallet fast and as he pulled out the money, and said, "I'm so sorry."

A few days later, I woke up and found my other car gone. I thought someone had stolen it and called the police; it turned out it had been repossessed. I then decided to have a yard sale, pulling everything out of my house except for Samuel's bed, and sold everything I could. Then I went and bought another car.

So, here we were sitting on the floor; I was still trying to figure out what I was going to do. I paid rent for a few months, bought food to fix for my son, and was trying hard to get it together. I felt so alone.

A few months later, I was getting very sick, throwing up; I couldn't eat or keep anything down. My mother came to check on me and asked, "What's going on? You don't look very good."

I told her I didn't know what was wrong; maybe it was having to deal with everything right now. After another week of my being sick, she talked me into going to the doctor. I made an appointment and went in for a checkup, with blood test and the works.

Mom went in with me. As I was lying on the bed still in my gown, the doctor walked in. He stood right beside me and patted my shoulder. He said with a big smile, "I have good news for you! You're going to have a baby- you're pregnant." I lay motionless. The doctor asked, "Is your husband in the waiting room?"

My mother turned around; she was as shocked as I was. She walked up to the doctor, pulled him aside, and I could hear her tell him, "Her husband was killed just a few months ago."

The doctor walked back to me and said, "I'm so sorry!" I felt a tear run down the side of my face. A million thoughts ran through my mind. He told me to get dressed and he would be right back.

I got dressed and sat down, still thinking, "I'm going to have another baby."

The doctor came back into the room and sat down in front of me. He said, "I spoke to your mother about what happened. I know you have a lot of things to think about right now. But I want you to know there are other options for you." I looked up at him. He went on and said, "Under the circumstances, you might consider an abortion. You're not that far along yet, and with everything that's happened, an abortion might be the answer. After all, you're still young, and later after you get through all this, you can start over again and have another baby in the future."

I felt so confused at that moment. I turned around and walked out. My mother was waiting for me, and we walked away in silence. It wasn't long before she told me, "You should really think about what the doctor said. You should consider abortion." She said, "It's hard enough with one kid; having two kids won't be any easier." She went on talking, but my mind was a thousand miles away.

♪❀

Everyone thought I was pregnant from my husband, but no one knew the guilt I felt inside, gnawing at my heart after his death. You could see that we were like two ships on a great big ocean, going different directions. We hadn't been physical since about a year before he was killed. I couldn't give myself to him anymore; I'd become cold and closed off to him, right after I found out about the first few women. I knew who the baby's father was, but it was hidden inside and I told no one.

♪❀

We think we can hide the things we do, but nothing we do in secret is hidden from the eyes of God. There are always consequences to everything we do, whether good or bad.

♪❀

My mother dropped me off at home. I walked into the house, paid the baby sitter, and said good-bye. I sat in the corner of the floor and wept like a baby; holding my son in my arms so tight, I cried and cried. *Now* what was I going to do? It wasn't long before I would start to show, and an abortion was out of the question.

I was running out of money; I had no job, and who was going to hire a pregnant woman? I went to a place called WIC, and was able to get food for free through them for Samuel. One day I stopped at the gas station to fill my car with gas; guess who showed up? Yes- the man with the fancy car- Joe. He jumped out of the car and told me he'd heard what had happened to my husband, and asked if I was OK. I said, "Yes, I'm fine."

He asked if it would be all right to ask for my phone number; I gave it to him.

A few weeks later the phone rang; it was Joe. He asked, "Are you okay?"

I answered, "YES!"

Then he repeated, "Are you sure you're OK?"

I was silent. I felt a lump in my throat; I wanted to cry, but held in the tears, and hung up the phone. I was getting bigger it seemed, by the day. A few days later I heard a knock on my door, and when I opened up, once again it was Joe. I just stood there, and then he noticed my tummy. "Wow, you're pregnant." He noticed my house was empty, and asked if he could come in.

I said, "I don't have any chairs to sit on."

He walked in, and then asked, "How are you making it?"

I replied, "One day at a time."

He looked at my tummy again and said, "Whose baby?" I looked at him and said nothing.

I turned around because I felt like I was going to start crying, but I didn't want to cry in front of him- I didn't really know him. He came up beside me, and said, "Listen, I'm getting out of the Army. I'm leaving for California in a few weeks. Go there with me, let me help you."

I looked at him. I was empty inside. I was extremely broken and up against a wall, and he knew it.

"Listen- no strings attached. Let me help you!"

I was by now almost 6 months along. He said, "You can't live like this, with no furniture, no job, no money. Come with me to California, please!"

He said, "I'll be right back."

He left, and then came back, his arms filled with bags of food. He went into the kitchen, and as he started to cook dinner, he smiled and said, "I'm a pretty good cook, by the way."

I wanted to scream, "NO, NO, NO!" But I was broken, lost, and empty inside; I just sat and watched him cook.

He fixed dinner, we ate, and later he left, returning to his own place; he didn't try anything. The next day he called again, and said he had a few things for my son. Every night after work, he'd come over to make sure we were OK. He always brought milk and cookies for Samuel. The time came for him to leave for California. He asked me again, "Please! Luauna, PLEASE come with me."

My month's rent was coming up, and I was completely out of money. The ugly and vicious cycle of sin, the curse of generations, was slowly taking its course. I said yes, I would go with him. Joe seemed very nice; he watched over my son and me. I emptied my house, sold almost everything except what I needed. We were packed and on the road, leaving Colorado and headed for California, a place where I'd never been. We found a little house, unpacked, and I found myself setting up as if we were husband and wife. Everyone around us thought we were married, and I was getting closer to term.

Something happened, though: I felt sick, weak, and dizzy, and felt a great deal of pain at the bottom of my belly. I went to the doctor, who told me, "The baby's trying to come, but it's too early."

I was given total bed rest, while Joe took care of us. I was in and out of the hospital, till it was time to deliver. I shared with the doctor how I couldn't have my son because of my hips had been broken. He said, "We'll need to take the baby by caesarian section." A date was set, and before you knew it, I was having a baby. I was still awake during the delivery, and all I heard was, "It's a girl," then an amazing cry came out.

As I felt a tear swell up, I said, "Please let me see her." They wrapped her tight in a blanket and laid her on my chest. Something started to happen- I heard the doctor say, "Help me! We have a problem." Almost immediately they placed something over my mouth and nose and I was *out*; I was hemorrhaging and lost a lot of blood.

When I woke up, again I felt like I'd been run over by that same Mack Truck as when I had Samuel. I felt so sick, but then they brought me my new baby girl.

Again, I opened the blanket, and counted those tiny toes. She was exquisite! The nurse walked in and smiled. She said, "She sure is beautiful. Do you have a name for her?"

I hadn't even thought about a name, and answered, "No."

Still smiling, the nurse said, "No hurry."

I was alone in that hospital room, holding this sweet baby girl in my arms. Perfect, she was perfect! I smiled as I held her in my arms, and told her, "Welcome to my world, little one." I started to cry; I didn't know why, but I couldn't hold back the tears. I wept in her blanket, holding her tight in my arms, looked at her, and thought, "I'm sorry little one; it's been so crazy I haven't thought about a name. You are so beautiful, and so special."

Later the nurse came in and asked if I was all right. I half smiled and nodded my head, trying hard not to start crying again. This nurse was very kind; she walked up beside me, and her gentle voice assured me, "It's gonna be okay; you'll see! Your baby is beautiful and precious."

I looked at my little girl's gorgeous big, dark eyes; they were almost black. I kissed her forehead and agreed, "Yes, she is." Then as I looked up, I read a name in golden bronze on the wall outside my door. I asked the nurse, "How do you pronounce the word over there in the hall, outside my door?"

She answered, "Kaweah; it's Indian. It's the name of the hospital you're in." I hadn't even realized the name of the hospital. She further explained that there was also a river in the area called Kaweah. She then asked me, "Aren't you Native American?"

"Yes, Apache!" was my reply, "Do you know what Kaweah means?"

She said, "I have been told it means, 'purity and strength'." She walked out of the room because someone was calling on her.

I lay in my bed thinking, "Purity and Strength..."

Later, when the nurse returned to my room to clean up the baby, I asked her, "Are you the one I need to speak to about writing down my baby's name?"

She called someone on the spot. A nurse from the nursery department came into my room while the first nurse was still washing the baby. "So you've decided on a name?" she asked.

I was excited to say, "Yes! Her name will be, Kaweah Angel Stines; Kaweah, because she will be great in strength. Her middle name will be Angel because she looks like a little angel, and because she is so pure. That's her name, Kaweah Angel Stines."

The first nurse smiled again, and said, "I like that name."

It wasn't long before I was out of the hospital, moving pretty slowly, but- at least I was moving. My life was now filled, caring for two babies: a toddler and a newborn.

꧁ꕥ꧂ꕥ꧁ꕥ꧂ꕥ꧁ꕥ꧂ꕥ꧁ꕥ꧂ꕥ꧁ꕥ꧂ꕥ꧁ꕥ꧂ꕥ꧁ꕥ꧂ꕥ꧁ꕥ꧂ꕥ꧁ꕥ꧂

I wasn't back home long, before the "no strings attached" condition was forgotten...

You can't live under the same roof without opening the door to temptation. It's as if you dunked yourself in a bucket of blood, then gone swimming in an area that's shark infested, thinking that nothing will happen...

That first shark gets a good sniff of the blood, and - **CHOMP!** *- then you're torn apart. Let's not forget the scripture, Roman 6:23: "For the wages of sin is death..."*

꧁ꕥ꧂ꕥ꧁ꕥ꧂ꕥ꧁ꕥ꧂ꕥ꧁ꕥ꧂ꕥ꧁ꕥ꧂ꕥ꧁ꕥ꧂ꕥ꧁ꕥ꧂ꕥ꧁ꕥ꧂ꕥ꧁ꕥ꧂

I felt trapped again, and the feeling of emptiness grew; not being in love with this man made everything worse. Yes, it was my own fault! I thought to myself, "Maybe something will change in my heart", but you can't live *outside* of God's will and expect things to work. After a while I noticed something happening. He was a hard worker, the first time I saw him nodding out, I thought he was merely tired from work. It wasn't long before I discovered he was a heroin addict. He was a very strong man, fearful of no one. It was nothing for him to fight anyone who stood in his way, and he always packed a gun. I found myself getting scared, as Joe sunk deeper and deeper into his addiction.

One day, I asked myself, "What am I doing? I'VE GOT TO GET OUT OF HERE."

I saved money through yard sales, selling everything I didn't need, until I had enough funds to pay for a bus ticket. One day I packed a few bags, left a note, and had a neighbor take me to the bus station; I was headed back to Colorado Springs. It took almost three days, which seemed like a week with two little ones in tow. I had enough money to rent a small house, and started looking for work right away. I found a little Mexican woman, who needed a place to live, and we worked it out; she would babysit while I went to work.

♪❀

I was determined to make it. I had always wanted to be a lawyer for some reason, I went to the college and asked what courses I needed to take towards a career as an attorney. They helped me line up classes, and I started right away. I also needed to work to pay the rent and buy food, I took a job as a waitress. But that didn't last long; I hated the way the men would speak, "Hey, Baby!"

I found myself glaring back at them and yelling, "I'M NOT YOUR BABY!"

On my day off, I went to a pancake street breakfast, downtown. As I sat on a bale of hay, I noticed a huge crane up in the sky; looking up I saw a team of men, hard at their job. I jumped up and walked over to the location where the big crane was. I saw a man with a white helmet on. He had the crane started, and was getting ready to move forward. I whistled from the ground and got the driver's attention. He opened his door, looked down at me and yelled over the engine, "HOW CAN I HELP YOU?"

I yelled back, "SHUT THAT THING OFF SO YOU CAN HEAR ME." He grinned, and shut it off. When he turned and looked at me, I yelled, "SIR, I NEED A JOB, I'M A SINGLE MOTHER. I'M A HARD WORKER. IF YOU GIVE ME A CHANCE YOU WON'T REGRET IT. PLEASE!"

He climbed down and looked me up and down. He shook his head; of course, I was a skinny little thing, wearing white shorts, white sandals, and a light blue color button-up shirt. I didn't give him a chance to say no. I said, "Sir, I am a hard worker. I'm not afraid of heights. Anything those men can do, I promise you; I will keep up with them and work hard."

He looked at me, then said, "I don't believe I'm doing this, or why! - but be here tomorrow morning at 7 am, and make sure you have blue jeans, boots- and get some gloves."

"Thank you, sir!" I was smiling from ear to ear.

"I've got to get back to work. See you in the morning, and DON'T BE LATE!"

I turned to walk away, then about-faced and yelled up to him "SIR, IS THE PAY MORE THAN WAITRESSING?"

He smiled again, shook his head and yelled back, "I THINK SO!"

I went to the thrift store and bought some coveralls and boots. The next morning, bright and early with gloves in hand, I was ready for work. I worked with a demolition crew, tearing down a big building called, "The Bicentennial," right in the middle of downtown Colorado Springs.

Going to school at night, working during the day, things were looking up, or so I thought.

❧❧❧❧❧❧❧❧❧❧❧❧❧❧❧❧❧❧❧❧❧❧❧❧❧❧❧❧

I was working hard, and excited about that first paycheck. Money was now coming in, and I felt all was well. Months went by- believe you me, I worked hard! I took evening classes at college, thinking that one day I would be a lawyer. For a while my schedule was go, go, and then--- go. I found my body getting tired; I was burning the candle at both ends. Although I made a few friends at work, I was the only woman, I was cautious. One day a coworker said to me, "You look tired."

I explained to him that I was going to school at night, and then working a full day, and how my two kids kept me going nonstop. He said, "I have something that will give you a little energy." He held out his hand, gave me two little white pills, and said, "These keep me going 24/7."

I asked, "What are they?"

He smiled, and said, "They're GOOD! 'White Cross - they're speed."

He got up and walked back to work; I was dragging, but scared to take what he gave me. Then later I thought, "I will break it in half, to try it."

It wasn't long before I had a surge of energy; I was up and running from one place to another with ease. Later that night, I thought, "Wow, that was only half the pill." The next morning I decided to take a whole one, and again I was moving with ease. It wasn't long before I found myself asking if he had more of those little white pills.

Months went by, and every day I was taking White Cross. One day an old friend walked up, looked at me, and asked, *"Girl, what are you taking?"* I grinned and replied, "Nothing."

He asked me again; I told him, "Just a little bit of speed." What he didn't know was that I was buying jars ("Lots") of speed, selling some, and using the rest.

"Speed kills! It has strychnine in it. In time you'll lose those teeth." Then, "You should use cocaine instead. It does the same thing."

"I don't use a needle."

"Girl, it's powder, you snort it. Here, try it!" He gave me an ounce of cocaine, and the following day I tried it.

I sold all the speed I had, and was now using cocaine. I made good money, and worked hard. My habit was growing, but I couldn't see the trap. I worked hard during the day, and went to school at night. The building was about done, and the next building to be torn down was unknown. My boss wanted me to continue working with them, but there would be a few weeks off before we'd know the next location. It was a hard job, and my body could feel it- ouch! During the break, I found some information about the Barber College and went in to speak to someone about it.

I asked, "How much money do you make? How long does it take to finish school?"

When I found out you could make really good money if you worked hard, I decided it would be much easier than the hard labor I was doing.

I signed up and paid for my school from the money I'd made. I loved it! Hairstyling was like art, and I found I was a natural at it. In time I was having a blast, being out on the floor and cutting hair. My instructors watched me closely because they were thinking of training me for hair competitions. I remembered seeing their entire collection of trophies in the office. Later, I found out that they were training for the World Competition in Japan.

One day my instructor, Don, asked me to stay after class; the instructors wanted to talk with me. They told me that I had a gift with my hands, and asked if I would allow them to train me that maybe one day I would be a part of their USA team. This was all wild, new, and crazy to me... hair shows?

"OK, whatever- I'll train!"

Training started right away; I was still cutting hair as a regular student, and stayed on cocaine. I was informed that I needed to compete in a few hair competitions, and must win first or second place for Colorado. I loved it, and the training came easily for me. I took second place for the state of Colorado, when the competition was held in Vail. This opened a whole new door for me: beauty, drugs, and wild living. A whole team would meet; after the competitions, everyone partied. Although I was very shy, I found that while I was high on cocaine I was a whole different person. I could talk without feeling insecure and withdrawn.

ᏕᎾ

Like a whirlwind, I was now in a different trap. Money was no longer a problem; I made plenty of it, and in time I was cutting hair and charging a good price for it. It wasn't long before this field opened another door: I loved music, and I loved dancing-late night dancing, high on cocaine. Having lots of money, I thought, "I am free, free to do whatever I want." I didn't have to answer to anyone, nor did I need to depend on anyone. I was a hard worker, made good money, and now I was buying a few homes.

One day a young Cuban gentleman came into the shop. I cut his hair and he liked it; as he paid me, along with the money he placed in my hand, I saw a paper folded into a small square. He said, "It's a tip."

I looked at him; he smiled and said, "Relax, it's only a little cocaine. You have tried it, right?"

I smiled and said, "Thanks!"

Sure enough, it was cocaine all right; it was some of the purest. Later he sent in his dad and brothers; before you knew it I was cutting hair for the whole family and getting paid VERY well. I discovered that they were major cocaine dealers, I kept some distance because I was a little bit fearful of them. I still did their haircuts, because I knew they'd supply my growing daily habit.

Without notice, I was starting to walk the same course as my mother had- the very same CURSE. Not so much with the men, but I was dancing, partying, doing drugs, and going out to the clubs; it was a normal thing for me. My kids were at home with a babysitter who now lived in my house, and without noticing, I was following in my mother's footsteps. In my mind I excused it and was blind because I figured I didn't bring men home like my mother had. *I* was somehow better.

Every once in a while the babysitter, Ester, would tell me someone named Joe had called. I knew who it was, but told her, "I don't want to talk to him. Whenever he calls, even if I'm home, tell him I'm *not home.*"

Almost two years had gone by since I'd left California, but it seemed like just yesterday. The days flew by. I was working to earn more money, buy homes, cars, fancy clothes, and all the things that are supposed to make you happy. One day was running into another; go to school, out at night- it was crazy! I was surrounded by gay men in the beauty field. They would always invite me to the gay clubs; after all, they had the best music, and besides, I felt safe. I loved to dance, and I had three dance partners. They were not gay; we were only friends who loved to dance.

One Friday, Ester told me that she and her family were going out for a few days to visit family. I needed a break anyway, I told her no problem. They left Friday afternoon after her husband came home from work. We said good-bye, and I made a list of the things I needed to get done Saturday and Sunday.

Then I put the kids down for the night, and went to bed too; I wanted to wake up early Saturday to complete my list.

The next morning, I made our breakfast, then sent the kids out to play in a small area they had in the backyard. Around 11 a.m., I brought the kids in to eat and get them ready for a nap, when I heard a knock on the door. I wasn't expecting anyone, and without thinking to look out the window, I opened the door...**Joe.**

My heart skipped a beat! I tried to close it fast, but he stuck his foot inside, so I couldn't shut and lock it. He was too strong for me. I turned and ran- down the hallway of the house into my room; I turned to lock the door, but it was already too late. He was pushing open the door. I ran to my bedroom window to open it and jump out, but he roughly jerked my head back in. When I tried to scream, I was thrown across the room. I tried to fight back, but just as fast as I lifted myself and tried to run out of the room, he threw me back across it. This time, I hit the wall and landed on the bed. Within seconds, he was sitting on me, with both hands wrapped around my neck. I reached up and tried to unravel his tight gripped fingers from around my neck. I couldn't breathe, and couldn't loosen his grip. He was leaning over me, staring down; his eyes filled with such hatred as he continued to choke me. I was getting dizzy, and I knew I was going to die.

I looked and saw from the side, that my son, only 4-1/2 years old, had come into the room and was trying to help me, jumping on the man's back, screaming, "Leave my mommy alone!" I looked up- my son Sam was still on this man's back screaming, "LEAVE MY MOMMY ALONE!"

Then everything went black...

I don't know how long I was out, but when I woke up, my son was weeping and trying to shake me. I could barely see Sam. I tried to catch my breath; I could barely breathe. I started to choke. My head felt like it was going to bust open. I tried to stand up and walk, but could barely raise myself, I was still trying to recover from the attack. I was afraid Joe was still in the house. I reached for the phone and dialed my mother's number. She answered, "Hello?"

I tried to talk but nothing came out; I could barely talk! All I could say was, "Mom, HELP ME!" In a raspy, scratchy voice I said it over and over, "MOM, HELP ME, HELP ME!"

Then I heard her ask, "LUAUNA! Is this YOU?"

I said, "YES, HELP ME."

She knew something was wrong, hung up the phone and was at my home in a moment's notice. She came right in and down the hall, and found me sitting in the corner, shaking, with my son and my daughter in my arms. My mother took one look at me, and shrieked, "OH MY GOD, WHAT HAPPENED TO YOU?

She started to cry and asked me, "Have you looked at yourself in the mirror?"

"No, I was too scared he was still in the house."

"WHO? Who did this to you?" She helped me walk into the front room, and as I walked into the room, looked at a mirror hung on the wall. I was shocked at what I saw! My face was swollen almost to the size of a basketball; the blood had come to the top of the skin surface all over my face, the whites of my eyes were beet red, and filled with blood. Not one bit of white could be seen in my eyes. My neck was red with his hand marks.

I stood looking in the mirror and started to weep. I still couldn't talk. As I sat down my mother again asked, "WHO DID THIS TO YOU?"

I whispered, "Joe. He is back from California."

My mother went to the phone to call the police, but I jumped up- "NO MOM," I whispered, "You don't know Joe. If he knows I called the police, he will kill me."

Tears were running down my face, and my Mom knew I was scared. She said, "If we don't call the police, he can still kill you."

I didn't know why I was still alive; maybe he thought he did kill me. I was scared of Joe; he was no one to mess with. Even though he was my daughter's father, this was one man I didn't need to be around. I couldn't go to work for a few weeks. My mother begged me to call the police, I was too scared of this man. I moved to a different house, then went out and bought a gun.

ANGER OF THE FOOLISH

6

Proverbs 22:24-25; "Make no friendship with an angry man, and with a furious man do not go, lest you learn his ways and set a snare for your soul."

I found myself looking over my shoulder every day, wondering if I would be found dead the next time. I bought a gun; there was no need to go far to find one. The minute I let a few people know I was looking, a friend came over and showed me a small nickel-plated handgun he had for sale. It had a clip with enough bullets to get my point across. They took me out on a deserted road called Gold Camp; we found a place to teach me how to fire it. I became a pretty good shot, able to hit the target.

The next step was to move. I got a P.O. Box, changed my phone number, and thought to myself, "Maybe it will be a little harder to find me," but I still kept looking over my shoulder; I was afraid of Joe and rightly so.

Fear couldn't stop me, however; I kept right on with what I was doing. I finished Barber College and entered hair competitions, winning two first places and one second place in three different competitions for Colorado. I trained for the U.S. competition, held in St. Louis, Missouri, and finished in second place for United States. It was only a matter of time and I would compete for World Competition, which would be held in Japan.

Since I'd won a few competitions, it became easier for me to charge higher prices for my haircuts, and that was just what I did. I started raking in the money, and I could buy whatever I wanted. I found myself thinking, "I don't need anyone." It was nothing for me to buy an outfit that cost $300-$500.

"Money," they say, "will make you happy!"

*No! - it fills a void only for a moment! Do you remember last year's Christmas gift? Most of you can't. Do you remember the first day you bought your first car? You shined that car like it was an idol, but now it's really not that important to you, other than getting you from one place to another. Amazing how we think things will fill our hearts with satisfaction. Without **Jesus**, it doesn't matter what one can buy. Nothing fills the void except Jesus Christ!*

I was dancing, and learning to fit into whatever crowd I wanted. The more cocaine I used, the more comfortable I was speaking to people. One day I would wear my black leather jacket and ride a Harley motorcycle. The next day I'd dress up fancy, and ballroom dance at a place called The Broadmoor in Colorado Springs. When I went to work, I met all kinds of different people: bank owners, realtors, police officers, attorneys, wild and crazy rockers- it didn't matter who or what type of people- as long as I did a line of cocaine, I could cover up my insecurity.

I didn't realize that I was covering up all the pain hidden deep inside of my heart. It wasn't long before I was like a time bomb. I became moody and very short tempered. One day ran into another. I'd rise up early to fix the kids their breakfast, and get them ready for the babysitter. I was short-tempered with my own children, and yelled at them for no reason. Sometimes I'd "scream" obscenities under my breath, echoing the same caustic words my mother had used. Tension was always in the air.

Off to work to make that money, lines of cocaine throughout the day. Later, I came home to spend time with the kids, make dinner and get them ready for bed. I had a live-in babysitter; once the kids were down for the night, I'd do another line of cocaine, get ready and dressed for dancing.

My fuse got shorter and shorter.

ᏚᎾ

One afternoon while I was driving down a main road in town, Nevada Avenue, a car pulled up beside me. Three girls were in their car and the music was blaring. One of them looked in my direction; she must have thought I couldn't hear her as she turned and told her friends, mocking, "It's a *spic* in the car next to us." Her other friends turned towards me and they all started laughing. It took me about a whole 3 seconds to yell out the window, "WHAT DID YOU SAY?" The light turned green and they drove off, with me right beside them. I yelled out the window, "I'LL SHOW YOU A *SPIC!*" I swerved my steering wheel; they pulled over and stopped, thinking I was going to ram their car. Without thinking, I jumped out of my car in a flash, opened the driver's seat door, pulled the girl out and started fighting right on the side of the road.

I turned to go after the other girls, but they started running. I jumped back into my car and drove off. After I'd left, and cooled down, it hit me: "WHAT WAS I THINKING?"

Something inside of me was happening; I was like a volcano getting ready to erupt. I found myself angry all the time. I didn't sleep much; only a few hours a night and my day would start all over again.

꧁꧂꧁꧂꧁꧂꧁꧂꧁꧂꧁꧂꧁꧂꧁꧂꧁꧂꧁꧂꧁꧂꧁꧂꧁꧂꧁꧂꧁꧂꧁꧂꧁꧂꧁꧂

One Saturday afternoon I was riding my motorcycle through a park, and noticed a policeman watching me as I passed by. I thought to myself, "I hope he doesn't pull me over," because I had a little cocaine in my pocket. Riding past him, I looked through my side mirror and there he was, riding up behind me. I went about two blocks out of the park; sure enough, he put his lights on. I felt my heart sink- I knew I wasn't speeding. I pulled over; he did the same, got out, and walked towards me. I asked right away, trying not to show that I was nervous, "Why did you pull me over, Officer?"

He asked for my driver's license, and proof of insurance. I got off of my bike, reached into my bags, and handed them to him.

Again, I asked him, "Why did you pull me over?"

Then he said something stupid, like "I thought your back light was broken."

I looked at him and said, "*Well it's not.*"

He looked at me, and smiled as he asked, "Is everything up to date on your driver's license?"

"Yes, of course it is."

I then found out the real reason he'd pulled me over: "Can we have coffee sometime?"

I felt my blood boil in seconds. I jumped back on my motorcycle, grabbed my license out of his hand, and rode off, yelling, "NO!"

I felt my heart almost pounding out of my chest; I was frightened he would pull me over and discover that I was high on cocaine. After catching my breath, I went home. My babysitter and her husband were going out of town for the night, so I stayed home. Later that evening, about 10 p.m., I heard a knock on the door. My heart skipped a beat; what was this person doing, coming to my house at this time? I wasn't expecting anyone. My kids were already sleeping. I ran to the bedroom, grabbed my gun, and crept into the front room, to look out the window. I couldn't believe it! - It was the policeman who'd pulled me over earlier that day. I was seething with anger. I held the gun to my side and had it ready. I didn't open the door, but looked out the window right at him and yelled, "WHAT THE %#@&*%# ARE YOU DOING AT MY DOOR?"

I kept yelling, "YOU SICK *%^#*$%, WHAT'S YOUR BADGE NUMBER? I'M TURNING YOU IN. YOU'RE **SICK!**"

He tried to calm me down, and said he was sorry. After I heard him start his pick-up line, "You were so beautiful today on that motorcycle", I yelled again, "YOU'RE SICK, YOU STUPID *%^#*$%- -- you pulled me over to get my address. I'M CALLING THE POLICE, YOU SICK PERVERT!"

I reached for the phone, opened the curtain on the window so he could see the phone in my hand. He turned around and walked away. I was shaking, scared, and paranoid, thinking, "What if he comes back? Do I call the police? If I do call the police, what if they send *him?*"

It was terrible that night; I couldn't sleep at all, thinking he was coming back. I was afraid to call the police, because by this time there were as much as six grams of cocaine in the house, and I kept a gram on me at all times.

Tormented in fear, paranoia, and short tempered: a vicious cycle!

ᔔᗜ

I looked like I had it all together on the outside, but inside I was in anguish. In the beauty field I hung around gay men. The places to dance were the gay bars filled with men, because I needn't worry about getting picked up; I was there because I loved to dance.

Wickedness was surrounding me; these demons of darkness were wrapping their tentacles deeper and deeper into my body: Drugs, Fear, and Anger. I was hanging with two sons of a major drug dealer; they were gay and we loved to dance. My cocaine supply was unlimited. I never slept; even my babysitter noticed I was changing. She would try to talk to me, but I was blind- in darkness. Month after month, making money, I didn't even have to buy my cocaine, because of my "generous" clients.

Clothes, cars, stereos, fancy rugs, shoes: whatever I wanted I bought. This went on for a few years. I didn't trust anyone and got close to no one. I went into the bar when it was late, and always knew when it was near the "bewitching" hour. That was what I called the end of the night when people were looking for someone to take home. I made it a habit to excuse myself, go towards the bathroom, and slip out the door. Then I would go find a cup of coffee somewhere, and return when it was "after hours". That was when the bar closed at 1:30 a.m., and they made everyone leave. Then they would reopen the doors at 2:15 a.m., and people could dance until 4 a.m.- *crazy!* - but I would go back and dance the night away. Thinking I had no care in the world. I would make it home in enough time to get a few hours of sleep, then up again, feed the kids, off to work. It was like I was in a whirlwind, going nowhere fast!

CRISTINGRISINGRISINGRISINGRISINGRISINGRISINGRISINGRISINGRIS

*Cocaine was a tool from **Hell**. The money was a pretend satisfaction; the anger was a rage of protection. I was a broken woman, running from all pain of my past, and scars of rejection. Trying to cover up with all the world says is supposed to bring one comfort, I was empty!*

I didn't know how to live, and I didn't know what love was.

CRISTINGRISINGRISINGRISINGRISINGRISINGRISINGRISINGRISINGRIS

Day and night, I had the same routine. One night a friend, Sofia, called and asked if I was going out to the club. "Of course!" I said, "It's Saturday night."

She told me she wanted to go out, but her babysitter wasn't available that night. I suggested, "Why don't I come over to your house, and my babysitter can watch all of our kids?" Problem solved.

While I was waiting for the babysitter to arrive at Dee's house, I finished my make-up and hair. We waited around for a while; I hated arriving at the club early. Normally, I drove by myself, but when Sofia asked if we could ride together, I said, "OK, sure, but I am driving my car."

While we were on our way to the club, she looked over at me and said, "Hey, want to stop by a friend's house? They're having a party." I looked at my watch, and she said, "We'll stop just for a little while, okay?"

I didn't know her friend, but it wasn't very late, we had a little time, and I agreed. We reached the house and parked; cars were everywhere. Entering the house, I saw people I had never met. Smoke filled the house. I thought, "Whoa, look at all this smoke."

As we made our way into the main room, the smell of smoke grew stronger and stronger. My eyes were starting to hurt from all the smoke. When I turned around to look at the people sitting everywhere in the front room, I realized it was *not* cigarettes, but marijuana smoke. Everyone looked wasted, with red eyes, and seemed to be out of their minds. Some of the people were laughing for no reason; they were in another world. Others appeared to be nodding out.

"It's too early in the evening for me", I thought. My friend was looking for the guy, Brad, she had been dating off-and-on; he was the one having the party.

She nudged me. "Come on."

We headed for the dining room, where there were about six people sitting around this table. Suddenly, my nose caught a different smell; I saw, lying on the table, syringe needles, spoons filled with little cotton balls, matches, and white powder.

For a moment I thought, "What am I doing in this place?"

It must have shown on my face, as Sofia looked at me and said, "Don't worry; we'll be here only for a little while."

I showed her an untrusting smile, and looked around just in time to see a young lady jump right in front of me. She sat on the chair in front of Brad, our host. He looked at her and asked, "OK baby, are you ready?"

He filled the spoon with the powder, added water and lit a match and heated the spoon. Then with a syringe needle in his hand he sucked up the stuff in the spoon, then put a tourniquet on her arm. After finding a vein, he shot the stuff into her arm. She slipped into another world, almost falling out of the chair, laughing. They put her with the group of other people who looked wasted.

I took a moment to tell myself, "Get out of this place!"

Unexpectedly, Brad looked at me and asked, "What about you, girl?"

I looked at him with a blank stare... then looked away. He went on to say, "What, you don't do drugs?"

Again, I looked at him with that same stare, as I thought to myself, "None of your business, buddy."

But he kept pushing the question, "What about you?" Brad laughed and said, "You don't know about drugs, do you?"

He wouldn't stop mouthing off and mocking me. Before he got anyone else's attention, I said, "I don't do needles."

He looked at me point blank; we were staring eye to eye. "What have you done?" he asked.

I looked at him and replied, "Cocaine."

"What, up your nose?" He asked, laughingly.

I replied, "Yeah, that's right."

"Baby, you are wasting it." I looked at him again with the same blank stare. He said to me, "Sit down", as he patted the empty chair in front of him. I just looked at him.

"Come on, girl," he said, "sit down. Relax and don't be so uptight." I sat down and he said, "Let me see your arms." Like a fool, I put my arms out for him to look at; he looked like a crazy man who'd found treasure. "Ooh- virgin veins, never been touched!" He rubbed my arms up and down looking like a mad man.

I pulled my arms away, and said, "Again, I do not do needles." As I sat there, he looked at me; with a weird smile, he pulled out of his pocket a clean needle wrapped in plastic.

"Look," he said, "this needle is clean. Come on; try a little cocaine in the vein, just a little..."

Foolish, and led into his trap, I put my arm out in front of me. He looked at me, grinning as he prepared the stuff. With the needle ready, he strapped up my arm; my veins showed strong, and in went the needle, but suddenly, something was happening! I started to feel a lot of pain, looked at my arm, and saw a strange ball. He looked a little scared, and said, "Oops, you have rolling veins." He worked hard and tried to find my vein again; again it slipped.

Pain shot up my arm. I thought to myself, "You don't know what you're doing."

He pulled the needle out; "Let me try the other arm," he said, and before I could do anything, my other arm was tied off fast; he stuck the needle into my other arm. Again my veins rolled, and then, all of a sudden I could feel something happening to my body.

I said, "Stop!" He did stop, and pulled the needle out; I could definitely feel something going on in my body.

I moved and sat in another chair. I wanted to leave. We stayed a little longer, till I finally told Sofia, "I'm leaving."

"Wait for me," she said, and we left.

Arriving at the club, we went into the bar. My heart was racing 90 miles an hour. I thought a glass of wine might calm me down. As I got my glass of wine, I took off my trench coat and placed it over one arm. I then reached for my wine glass with the other hand and started to walk around the outside area of the dance floor. I looked around for my dance partner; I saw him, hoofing it on the dance floor. I watched him as he moved; he was an excellent dancer.

As I looked around, my eyes caught the other people dancing. I found a corner in the room with a great view of the dance floor, and stood still, watching the people. For some strange reason, as I just stood there, it felt as if I were in a glass bottle with the lid closed. Looking at the people, it seemed like their smiles were fake. As I cast my eyes around, I noticed men trying to make their smooth moves on women; watching further, I noticed women making eyes at the men.

Funny, I had never seen the club in this manner before. The people looked phony; as I watched the dance floor and looked around the bar, everyone looked plastic. I caught Sofia's eye as she danced around with some other guy she spent the night with every now and then. She even looked different to me that night, as I saw the empty expression on her face; her eyes looked shallow.

I stood in that corner for what seemed like forever, but it was maybe only 30 minutes. I thought to myself, "Look at all these people! Wow, they look fake."

It was as if they were trying really hard to have fun. I walked around to the other side of the dance floor. My dance partner, Brian, said, "Girl, what is wrong with you? Are you OK? Come on, let's dance."

I still had my wine glass in one hand and my trench coat over my other arm, as I looked at him and said, "Not right now, I'm finishing my wine; go find someone else to dance with." He turned around and went on to find another partner.

I then caught Sofia's eye and told her, "I am leaving!"

She asked, "What? It's early!"

I looked at my watch; it was about 11:30 p.m. I said, "I am sorry, I want to leave."

I told her if she could find a way home I would pay the sitter and watch the kids at her house, so she could stay out as long as she wanted. I knew the kids were already asleep. I told her I would sleep at her house tonight. She asked me if I was sure; I smiled and said, "See ya, have fun."

I walked out the door of the club that night, not saying good-bye to anyone else. I drove to Sofia's home and paid the sitter. I went back into the front room and sat there on the couch. It was quiet; I took off my jacket, and rolled up the sleeves of my blouse- her house was hot!- when something caught my eye. Dark, purple bruises on my arms, both arms: it looked as if someone had beaten me up. Then out of my peripheral vision, I caught a glimpse of Sam and Kaweah, all snuggled in their sleeping bags; lying on the floor... they looked so innocent. I looked at my arms, and then looked at my kids' faces. Then it hit me like a ton of bricks: "How in the world did I get into this mess?"

I sat there on my friend's couch, looking at my children and then my arms. I started to think to myself, "What happened to me? What am I doing?"

Then it was as if I heard my friend's (the friend from the Seven-Eleven) words in my mind- who six to eight months earlier had tried to share Jesus with me. (That story is in *A Mother's Story*) Her words echoed through my mind, "Jesus loves you, and has a plan for your life."

I started to tear up as I sat alone in my friend's apartment. I did not know how to pray; I had never been to church.

I lifted my head and looked up, "God, are you there? Are you really up there?" I started to cry, "God! Can you see me? I don't know if you are real- I don't know what to believe! God, if you are real, then come right here and show me. I don't even know your name, Help ME, please! I am giving you three months, God; if you don't prove to me who you are, I will never ask you for another thing for the rest of my life."

Weeping, I went to lie down and fell asleep like a baby that night. Right to sleep...

THE WINGS OF AN EAGLE

7

Isaiah 40:28-31; "Have you not known? Have you not heard? The everlasting God, the LORD, the Creator of the ends of the earth, neither faints nor is weary. His understanding is unsearchable. He gives power to the weak, and to those who have no might He increases strength. Even the youths shall faint and be weary, and the young men shall utterly fall, but those who wait on the LORD shall renew their strength; they shall mount up with wings like eagles, they shall run and not be weary, they shall walk and not faint."

So... here I was the next morning, sitting in a beautiful historic church. You will recall what happened in the opening chapter.

That morning, I'd had a few mental battles as to where to go: what to wear, should I wear makeup? Do they wear their hair in buns? The only church I'd ever attended was at the Catholic orphanage where I'd spent a few years in my early childhood (Chapter Three). I didn't know how church people dressed or acted. But- it didn't matter; I was going to church.

I looked up the address to the one I'd been invited to, and headed out the door, not knowing what to expect; not knowing that this would be my last day as the Old Luauna, and my first step into new life in Jesus Christ; I've never gone back!

೧ಾಲ೧ಾಲ೧ಾಲ೧ಾಲ೧ಾಲ೧ಾಲ೧ಾಲ೧ಾಲ೧ಾಲ೧ಾಲ೧ಾಲ೧ಾಲ೧ಾಲ೧ಾಲ೧ಾಲ೧ಾ

Finding Jesus was truly finding the pearl of great price. The empty and dark hole: the void which was in my heart- my whole life was now gone. My heart was daily filled with love, joy, and peace instead; I'd found something I could never find before in the world.

೧ಾಲ೧ಾಲ೧ಾಲ೧ಾಲ೧ಾಲ೧ಾಲ೧ಾಲ೧ಾಲ೧ಾಲ೧ಾಲ೧ಾಲ೧ಾಲ೧ಾಲ೧ಾಲ೧ಾಲ೧ಾ

God's Word was growing deep within me. I was at every church service. You didn't have to call me, or beg me to come to church; I was sitting on the step waiting most of the time, for someone to open the door. I couldn't get enough of Jesus, and the church was where I was being filled. I wondered why we didn't have church every night. I read my Bible every day- morning, noon, and night. Sometimes I would fall asleep at night reading my Bible, and wake in the middle of the night with crumpled-up pages, from crushing the Bible in my sleep.

I would very carefully unfold the crumpled pages and lay it to the side of my bed; early in the morning I'd pick it up and start my reading again, for the new day! I must have read my Bible 3 times that first year as a Christian. It was like *life* pouring into my soul, reading with a dictionary on one side and a Strong's Concordance on the other, making sure I understood every word I read.

Something soared inside of me; the more I read the Bible, the more I felt myself jump right into the pages of this amazing book. It was as if I were standing with the young boy named David on the battlefield as he fought the giant Goliath, or I walked hand in hand with the three Hebrew boys as they were thrown into the fiery furnace.

I could imagine myself sitting upon the hill listening as Jesus shared the Word with the multitudes of people. I would find myself sitting at the table with Mephibosheth as David restored his life back to him. Hearing the words which brought tears to my eyes, God was speaking these very same words to me as I read II Samuel 9:78: "So David said to him, 'Do not fear, for I will surely show you kindness for Jonathan your father's sake, and will restore to you all the land of Saul your grandfather; and you shall eat bread at my table continually.' Then he bowed himself, and said, 'What is your servant, that you should look upon such a dead dog as I?'"

Knowing that I, too, was going to have my very life restored back to me...

I felt like I was there in each story of the Bible; reading to my children every night before bed, we soaked in every word written throughout the Bible.

One day while reading Matthew, Chapter 27, about the arrest of Jesus- His beatings, mocking, and how they nailed Him to the cross- those words reached out to grip my soul and heart. I sat in horror, tears running down my face. Laying my Bible to the side I fell to my knees, praying: "Jesus, I am so sorry for what they did to You. You allowed them to do all that; You went to the cross willingly, all because YOU love me, YOU love me!" I wept like a baby for hours thinking about God's love, His mercy, and His amazing grace.

Getting up that day from my knees, I knew I must be faithful to this amazing love.

I had only been saved 6 months at that moment, but I was determined to serve Jesus with all my heart. I had much to learn. Everywhere I went, and everywhere I looked, I saw people who needed Jesus; they needed this love. I found myself sharing Jesus everyday with someone; no matter where I went, all I wanted to do was tell people about Jesus.

♪❀♪❀♪❀♪❀♪❀♪❀♪❀♪❀♪❀♪❀♪❀♪❀♪❀♪❀♪❀♪❀♪❀♪❀♪❀

A year went by, and I was excited to learn more about Jesus every day. As I was walking out the door of church I saw a rack, filled with little books and tracts that shared Jesus in an easy form. I asked someone, "How much for the tracts?"

Smiling, she replied, "They are free."

I was surprised- FREE! She continued, "They are for anyone who wants to share Jesus."

I smiled and felt like I'd found a goldmine, and went through the whole rack, taking one of each. As I read them, I would look at the people to see who might match each tract, and give one to him or her.

At that time the church had about 100 people. When I found out they had prayer before each service, off to prayer I went. I cried out for the city of Colorado Springs every day; God placed His burden for the city in my heart. Everywhere I looked I saw broken people, single mothers, drug addicts, prostitutes, businessmen and women all in need of Jesus.

Little by little, I found myself working my way from sitting in the back row or balcony to the main floor, and in time I was sitting right in the front row. I wanted to sit in the front row, so I could find my way to the altar; it seemed like every service I needed to get something right in my heart. The Word was preached, and I didn't want anything hindering me from God's presence. With my notebook and Bible in one hand, and two kids in tow, I sat with daughter Kaweah on one side, and my son Samuel on the other, eager to learn at every church service. I didn't miss a service; I was there for both Sunday services,

Wednesday night, Morning Prayer, and Saturday outreaches. After all it was the least I could do for all that Jesus did for me.

I couldn't do enough; this love was filling my heart, and I knew it was the answer for many out there who were lost and broken without Jesus. It was on one Sunday evening after service during the second year I was saved, that I noticed a young woman sitting on the edge of the platform, tears streaming down her face. I was collecting all the kids' things; they'd fallen asleep during the service, I let them sleep as I carried their stuff out to the car.

I came back in to get the kids next; it was almost empty except for a few people. The young girl was talking to the assistant pastor; she said her mother threw her out. She wept uncontrollably as she was speaking. I was trying not to listen, but couldn't help overhearing the fear in her voice as she said, "What am I going to do? I'm a Christian now, my mother threw me out, and I have no place to go."

I looked down at the kids, so sweet and peaceful as they slept; picked up Samuel, carried him to the car, then walked back into the church to carry out Kaweah. The young girl was really crying now...

I *had* moved into a larger home with the kids...

I smacked *that* idea down: "I can't take her in; I don't like to live with anyone- it's me and my two kids- we're fine."

I was very much a loner, and this amazing walk with JESUS was all I wanted.

As I picked up my daughter to carry her to the car, I heard the pastor assuring her, "Listen, don't worry, we will find some place for you to sleep for the night." She was weeping like a baby, broken inside! Walking out the door, I turned to see her face. Those great big tears running down her cheeks touched my heart.

All of a sudden, I turned and said without thinking, "OK, she can stay with me for the night." I thought to myself, "WHAT DID I JUST SAY?"

I knew me! I hated my privacy invaded, but it was too late, because those words were already out. I stood there looking at them both, holding my baby girl in my arms. They both turned and looked at me. I said, "*Tonight* or maybe only a few days."

They both jumped up and the young girl came up to me, tears still streaming down her face as she was thanking me. That night was the beginning of God preparing me for ministry. The only thing was I didn't know it at the time.

A few days went by, and it seemed as if all these broken women, young and old, were coming in my path. What was God doing? I loved living alone; I was very picky, a neat freak. WHAT WAS HAPPENING? I remember the day like it was yesterday, while at a church service, the Holy Spirit was dealing with me to help these women. I fought it for a few days. One Sunday afternoon I was convicted again to help. Again, I made a million excuses. I told God, "Lord, you know I love to live alone, I am very picky, I am like a drill sergeant," on and on I went, one excuse after another, but the conviction wouldn't lift from my heart.

I had a good friend; she was very well off, and owned lots of property. Finally, I came to God with this proposition: "OK Father, I'll make a deal with You; if You want me to open a women's home, then you'll have to give me the right home. I have two children, and I want to have room for them, not to be uncomfortable (It was really *me* who didn't want to be uncomfortable)." I finalized the deal, "OK! If my friend has a house that's big enough, and cheap enough- *only then* will I know that it's You."

I rode my bicycle to her house after church. "Hoping she wasn't home," I knocked on her door, which was one of those huge Victorian houses on a street called Cascade Avenue in Colorado

Springs. As I turned to walk away, the door opened. She smiled and said, "Luauna! What a wonderful surprise to see you at my door."

I smiled back, and shared with her, "Well, I'm *sure* you probably don't have anything available, and that's OK, you can say NO, it's OK, and it probably will cost too much anyway, that's OK!"

"Luauna!" she asked, amused, "What do you need?"

I told her how I was thinking about starting a Christian home to help women, and single mothers with kids. I said, "I need a big house, but if you don't have anything it's OK."

She smiled again and replied, "I think that's wonderful; I happen to have Big Blue available right now."

I said, "But I'm sure it will cost too much rent each month and that's OK!"

She asked, "Well, how much can you afford?"

I smiled back, trying hard to get out of this "women's home" idea, and answered, "Not much!"

Right away, she reached from her side and handed me a key: "Here's the key to Big Blue, $400 a month, and don't worry about a deposit. See you later; we'll fill out papers next week."

After cheerfully handing me the key, she walked away to get ready for a meeting she needed to attend.

"What am I getting myself into?" I thought while riding my bike to the property.

Big Blue; that was a fitting name! In front of me was a big, beautiful blue Victorian 1898 house with 10 bedrooms. It had three stories, with two stairwells. The main stairwell in the front and another towards the back of the house; years ago the back stairwell would have been for the servants. I walked through the whole house checking out every room, opening every closet. After walking through the whole house, I walked again up the front stairwell and sat down on a step close to the second floor. Looking out a stained glass window, I asked myself, "Can I really do this?"

I placed my head into my lap, and started to weep as I prayed, "Lord, I don't know if I can do this. I don't trust anyone. I'm so picky. I am used to living with only the kids and myself. Jesus, I am scared; what if I fail? What if I can't love these girls the way You do?"

Did I hear thunder, or see lightning from heaven saying, "You can do it"? Or a voice telling me, "I'm sure you can?" NO! Not one word, but I knew it was the right thing to do. I rode my bike home, washed my face, and got ready for the Sunday evening service. That night in church, I felt God's sweet presence; His love was filling me up. I wanted to stay in His presence all night long.

After service, I went up to the assistant pastor, and told him that I was going to open a women's Christian home; I think I shocked him. It was simply a matter of time, and my kids and I were all moved in and unpacked. Sam and Kaweah loved this great big place, running up and down both staircases, exploring the whole house.

⁂⁂⁂⁂⁂⁂⁂⁂⁂⁂⁂⁂⁂⁂⁂⁂⁂⁂⁂⁂⁂⁂⁂⁂⁂⁂⁂

Well, to my surprise, in no time my first women's home was filled with 17 women and 5 children. What started with 17 girls, in time expanded into a second home, then a third home for women; they were called *Victorious Homes for Women*. I worked hard, and by God's grace He took care of all our needs.

I taught the women the Bible every week. I woke them for Morning Prayer at 6 a.m., every day of the week. I spent many hours a night counseling and encouraging these amazing women. Each one came from a different background: broken homes, sexual abuse, physical abuse, divorced; some were just released from prison. Each woman God brought into the home grew stronger in Jesus and His Word. We ate together every night like a big family; we laughed together, cried together, and even had a few "good old" fights.

I loved it! Was it trying at times? YES indeed! - But lives were being changed and touched for Jesus, and nothing else mattered.

SHE LEFT EVERYTHING

8

John 4:28-29: "The woman then left her water pot, went her way into the city, and said to the men, "Come, see a Man who told me all things that I ever did. Could this be the Christ?"

The women's homes were growing and doing well. I made rules for all of them. All church services were mandatory, and everyone must attend the weekly meetings. Morning Prayer was an absolute must; there was no way you could have 18-20 women living in the same house with only two bathrooms and NO PRAYER! Everyone had daily chores, and two women would be teamed up each night to cook dinner, once a week. We all ate together every night, except Saturday and Sunday. Those were free nights- pizza, popcorn, or Taco Bell.

I worked very hard to be the mother my kids needed as well. I never allowed anyone to come before my kids, Sam and Kaweah. This was very important to me; I never wanted them to feel like they were second place. If either of them had a problem or needed to ask me a question, they knew they could come to me and ask anytime.

My first two years of being a Christian, I read all of Dr. James Dobson's books on raising children. I wanted to break *every* curse and bad habit I'd learned; everything I'd done to raise kids the wrong way. I wanted no part of what I learned growing up. I wanted my son and daughter to have something I didn't have: *An opportunity to live a life in Jesus Christ, free from the bondages of this ugly world.*

♪❦

Learning to juggle everything was hard at first, but after a while, I realized I loved what I was doing! Ministering to women was a joy; I had the privilege of helping them grow into a vision for a better tomorrow. Every month, new women were coming in. We were excited about Jesus. The ladies and I were on the streets sharing Jesus, and we were filling the church up fast. Our women's home was at almost every outreach. After a while leading our women's home was like second nature; some women were being discipled into leadership.

Bible Conferences were held every six months, and I'd take time off to attend. This was a time where pastors of all ages, who were sent out to pioneer new churches, could come back to the home church; they'd gather together and share their war stories and victories. It was exciting. The first Bible Conference I attended gave me a whole new list of pastors' names to pray for during my Morning Prayer.

Later I got involved in choir and a Christian band; my whole life was wrapped in Jesus and church was amazing. I loved every bit of it.

♪❦

It was my third year: the Bible Conference was coming again, and I took time off all three days to make sure I attended every service. Each speaker spoke on the message, "WHO WILL GO?" Every speaker who was invited to speak at the conference preached about reaching the world for Jesus. Every altar call, I stood up to answer the call, "YES LORD, send me, I'll GO."

I remember like it was yesterday, my heart was stirred; each message touched my heart more and more. Praying faithfully every day, I decided that I was going to reach out even more for Jesus. I had a van, and decided I would go to the Red Cross Shelter every Sunday to find people in need of Jesus and who wanted to go to church.

Later, I also stopped at a place called Comcor, a rehabilitation center for ex-convicts. Filling up my van with those great big thugs made me smile every week. They would all pile into my van, squeezing in like a can of sardines, and then off to church we would go! My kids would get to church early to save about 10 seats for every service. The women's home was only a few blocks from church; the ladies were also walking there, I didn't worry about the kids getting to church on time.

Then we- all of us "thugs"- would walk into the church, all the way to the front row, to sit down. Every service I prayed and wondered who was going to come to Jesus. The girls from my home were very funny! - I'd often catch one of them peeking at the altar each service, wondering if maybe one of those mighty big brutes who gave his heart to Jesus just might be her future husband. Our church was steadily growing; a couple hundred people were now coming to church. Ministry was so much fun, and to be even a little part of its growth was such a privilege.

꒰꒱꒰꒱꒰꒱꒰꒱꒰꒱꒰꒱꒰꒱꒰꒱꒰꒱꒰꒱꒰꒱꒰꒱꒰꒱꒰꒱꒰꒱꒰꒱꒰꒱꒰꒱

I was steadily growing in the Word of God, and was excited about Jesus. During the first year I was saved, I remember a man of God, an evangelist, who came to visit the church; every one called him Pastor Eddie. At that time I was still sitting in the back row of the church. At the end of the service he stood and called a few people forward. I didn't really know what he was doing, or what it meant to give a prophetic word. He stopped, looked towards my direction, and called out, "The lady with the black dress."

I remember turning BEET RED; I knew *I* had a black dress on, but I thought, "PLEASE DON'T BE ME." I turned around, as if I were looking to find some other lady in a black dress. I was in the back row, trying not to make eye contact with Pastor Eddie because I was shy and insecure. Then he said- "YOU! Stop looking around, I'm talking to you." By this time I could feel every eye turn towards me. I turned and looked at him. He continued, "YES, YOU!" I pointed to me, and he said, "Yes, come up front." I felt like I was going to die!

I made my way towards the front of the church; the evangelist stopped, looked at me, and was silent for a moment. Then he went on to tell me: ***"You have been forsaken as a young wife, broken in spirit. But one day, you shall proclaim His Word beyond the waters of this land, for the Lord will restore the years of the cankerworm and the palmerworm. He, the Lord has called you, and He will make a way for you this day, says the Lord."***

At that time I didn't know what he meant, nor did I catch everything he said. A lady walked up who had written it down for me. She smiled and said, "Keep this; one day you will understand, that's a word from the Lord."

I was now going to these Bible conferences every 6 months, not thinking about a thing, just loving Jesus.

Something was happening inside my heart... It was around my fourth year, and one Sunday before church, during a Bible lesson, they showed a film called, "God's Generals". As I watched the film, something pierced my heart; I wanted to jump up and run to the altar. I was waiting for an altar call- I knew I needed to pray! – but at the end, they didn't give one, because it was time for the regular Sunday morning service.

All through that regular morning service, I kept waiting for the altar call; I *wanted* to *pray*. The second they said, "Every head bowed," I remember almost running to the altar; I got on my knees in the corner. I remember weeping and praying, "Father, I don't have anything much to offer you, but I'm available for Your service."

Although I cannot explain everything in detail, during that same moment I knew that morning that the Holy Spirit called me, and anointed me. I prayed for a little while, even though everyone was leaving because service was over. I wiped the tears from my eyes, and went home and prayed again.

I was so excited inside! I didn't know how, or when; I knew He'd called me. I started reading my Bible more. I figured if I'm going to be used by God I will need to know my Bible. I was still cutting hair; by this time I had my own barbershop to make extra money so I could help send out monies to preach the gospel.

I'd now been a Christian for six years. I was close to my pastor, and cut his hair for free every time he needed a haircut. I decided to ask him when he came in for his haircut, "What do I need to do to prepare to be a preacher?" The first time I asked him, "Do I need to go to Bible school to become a preacher? What do I need to do?"

He smiled and said, "Keep doing what you're doing."

This same response was given to me for about two years. Then one day I asked him, "What about becoming a missionary? Send me to Africa. My kids and I love Jesus; we'll go into Africa and start a church."

He'd just smile. I told him, "I'm serious! I feel God has called me to preach. Every time we have a Bible Conference we are asked 'who will *go*?' And every Conference I stand up in front, praying to go."

For the first time, he said, "You need to wait."

"Wait for what? I love Jesus; I have now been saved over 8 years, I have the women's homes going, and they're doing great. Do I need to go to Bible school?"

"*Bible school,*" he laughed mockingly, "Bible school, you'll only come out of Bible school twice dead, plucked up by the roots. Everyone I know that came out of Bible school came out *dead* spiritually."

I looked at him, thinking to myself in horror, "Well, in that case I don't want to become spiritually dead."

He continued: "Besides, I don't think that women should preach."

I was finishing his haircut when he said those words, but when I heard those words it was like a sword pierced right through the center of my heart. He noticed my expression, said, "You need to read Timothy!" thanked me for the haircut and walked out the door.

I reached for the broom to clean up the shop, and felt a tear well up. I didn't have any more appointments, I finished cleaning, locked the door, and sat in my barber chair. I opened up my Bible and read Timothy. I'd read I Timothy and II Timothy hundreds of times before. Yes, I did read where Paul speaks to young Timothy in I Tim. 2:11-12; "Let a woman learn in silence with all submission, and I do not permit a woman to teach or to have authority over a man, but to be in silence."

I read it over and over again that day, thinking, "Holy Spirit, how can this be?"

I started to study my Bible more and more. I didn't want to get out of God's will and try preaching if God said women couldn't preach.

LIKE A FIRE SHUT UP IN MY BONES

9

Jeremiah 20:9: "Then I said, 'I will not make mention of Him, nor speak anymore in His name.' But His word was in my heart like a burning fire shut up in my bones; I was weary of holding it back, and I could not."

I continued to be faithful in church, and in reading my Bible; the women's home was growing. I reached out to bring people to church every day. This was my life, yet the pastor's words, "Women can't preach," kept running through my mind. I am going to share some personal stories about my dating experiences in the church I attended, because they directly relate to this issue, as you will see later on...

One day a handsome young man asked me out for coffee. I hadn't really *dated* as a Christian, but this man was faithful to church, and he loved Jesus. His name was Scott; what a wonderful spirit he had! I hadn't dated a Christian man before, and this was new for me. I had great male and female friends at this church fellowship, but we all just hung out together;

going to coffee or getting pizza as a group, sometimes out for a hike.

Sometimes we'd all meet at the women's home for dinner on a Friday or Saturday night. I hadn't met anyone I wanted to date; I was busy with my kids, the ladies' home, and had my own business by this time.

A few men had asked me out, but I hadn't been attracted to them; I wasn't looking for a husband. Scott was different, though; he was quiet, kind, sweet, and I didn't see him trying to "rap" to all the girls. I'd see him in the prayer room before every church service. When we passed, he would smile, nod his head, and say hello.

I hadn't even thought about dating anyone at the time Scott asked me out, but I decided to go with him. Our first night out was amazing; he had me laughing hard, and we had so much fun. It wasn't long before he asked me out again to dinner, then another time for lunch. In time we'd go bike riding, and enjoyed being around each other. He respected me, and I loved this respect. We talked sometimes until after midnight, sitting in his car parked in front of my house. Even though we both knew we had to go to work in the morning, it didn't matter- we liked each other's company!

I hadn't told him of all I'd gone through, but his kind and gentle nature was something I had never experienced before. We were like two peas in a pod, hanging out like a couple of teenagers. One day he said, "I want you to meet my mother and father."

They lived in Minnesota. I felt very nervous; the man had never been married, and I had two kids. He smiled and said, "I really want my mother and father to meet you and the kids." I decided that we'd all go to meet his family in Minnesota. Scott was so kind, and his gentleness stunned me. He loved my kids, and Sammy really liked him. They would play football, talk about nothing, and sometimes Scott would show Sammy wrestling moves, because Sammy was on a wrestling team at school, and I think Scott wrestled when he was younger, in school. Kaweah really liked Scott as well.

We arrived in Minnesota and I was scared to death to meet Scott's family. It didn't take long to discover why Scott was kind. His mother and father welcomed my kids and me with open arms. They were truly a Christian family; a husband and wife married many years. They really loved and respected one another. I had never seen this before in my life, except as a child with my grandfather and grandmother.

I watched Scott's family. The whole week we were with them, we went camping, fishing, and hung around the house drinking coffee and laughing until late at night. They brought out their photo album and shared all the funny pictures of Scott and the whole family. I had never seen so much love in a family before. This was the first example of a true Christian family filled with God's love.

I remember towards the end of our visit, the night before we were to return, I was lying in my bed with the kids. I thought to myself, "What am I doing here? This family is too good for me."

I knew my background, and I hadn't shared everything with Scott. I was used to rejection, and I assumed he wouldn't want to be around me if he knew everything about my life, especially since he came from such an amazing family.

I was like a hidden, closed book; still insecure and feeling like I didn't deserve to be a part of this wonderful family. I didn't know how to love and I didn't know how to open up and share those thoughts with Scott, even though I had been saved for a few years by now.

When we returned to Colorado, it was back to work, and time for my pastor's haircut. I told him that I was dating Scott; he smiled and said, "I know."

I asked him that day what he thought about Scott and me dating.

"Scott is a good guy," he said, "but Scott's not the one for you; he won't do anything for God." He repeated, "I don't think he's the one for you."

I felt my heart sink. I didn't say much more that day, and finished up his haircut. Later, I thought to myself, "The pastor's probably right; I'm not good enough for Scott."

I broke up with Scott and stopped seeing him. I broke his heart, and mine, but couldn't tell him what the pastor said. Nor could I tell him what the devil was saying to my mind: that I wasn't good enough for him. Scott tried to talk to me, but he didn't understand. I didn't know how to talk things out.

For the record: Scott is an incredible man of God, whom I will always love and respect with all my heart. He is still a great friend of mine.

I continued doing what I knew to do, with the women's homes doing well. I kept reaching out, and I also helped start up a men's home. Laboring for the kingdom of God kept my mind busy. One day on an outreach, I ran into a man and his wife, who were about 60 years old. They asked me why I was sharing Jesus. I smiled and told them how my husband had been killed, that I was a single mother raising two kids, and how much I loved Jesus. They looked at each other, smiled, and asked me, "Would you please come and share your story with our group of men and women?"

"Sure," I replied, "I would love to, as long as it's not conflicting with my regular church time."

They invited me for a Friday night. I found out that they were in charge of a group of men and women for the Salvation Army. They introduced me, and I went up to share my story. Something happened that night; I felt heaven open, and the Holy Spirit filled the whole room. Men and women were saved, weeping and coming forward to the altar. I just stood there; the couple in charge came forward and asked me to please pray for each one who'd come forward. I prayed for everyone that night, and left with a big smile on my face. Before I left, they handed me an envelope. I opened it and saw a check made out to me. I looked up at them and asked, "What is *this* for?"

"It's an offering," they said, "for you!"

Handing it back to them, I said, "I can't take this! I didn't do this for money."

They smiled at me, handed back the envelope, and replied, "Always keep that spirit. You're sharing for Jesus. Please take it, and use it for you and the kids."

I ended up going once a month to share Jesus. WHAT FUN!

ॐॐॐॐॐॐॐॐॐॐॐॐॐॐॐॐॐॐॐॐॐॐॐ

I didn't know all that was happening, but God was opening the doors for me to share my story in different places. I made sure I never went to speak on a day or night when we had a church service. I found myself "sneak preaching." I couldn't share with anyone else other than Jill, who asked if she could go with me. It was sad, not being able to share all God was doing, lives touched and changed for Jesus, but the joy of the Lord was bubbling up inside of me.

I decided to return to the Zebulon Pike Detention Center to see if I could share my story with the kids who were locked up, like I'd been before. The opportunity opened and a meeting was set up. *Wow,* all the kids in the meeting were weeping and asking Jesus to be their Lord and Savior. I was filled up with God's love when I left that place, once again seeing lives saved and changed by the power of the blood of JESUS.

৵৽

It had been awhile since I'd broken up with Scott; he was now married and having children, and I was happy for him. Another man asked me out for coffee, and I accepted: His name was Darryl- he was amazing! We both loved to fish, hike, ride bikes; we had so much in common. Of course, we were both strong-willed, and had a few good arguments; we dated for over three years. We talked about marriage, and one day Darryl surprised me with a ring. I loved him with all my heart. We were good friends; he made me laugh so hard at times, my tummy hurt. Every time I thought about him, my heart would skip a beat.

As we were getting closer to setting a date to be married, I told him that I really wanted to preach. He shared with me how he wanted to join the military. He wanted to train for Special Forces, eventually to become a Green Beret. We cared a great deal for one another, but I didn't know how we could make it work. I thought at the time, he had to be a preacher or I couldn't preach.

In the church we were in, they taught that men were the ones who were to preach. How could our relationship work, with the thoughts we both had planted in our minds? It couldn't work! That's what we were taught: *"Women don't preach."* He knew I wanted to be in the ministry. I asked my pastor about Darryl, and to my surprise once again, he said, "Not Darryl; he's not for you, Luauna."

Then I heard the same thing he'd said about Scott, "Darryl won't do anything for Jesus."

I wanted to say at that very moment, "But *I'm* the one called to preach, not him," but I didn't say it out loud.

There was such a battle going on in my heart after those words were spoken. I didn't want to make God mad. I wanted to listen to my pastor. I knew I wanted to preach, and even though I loved Darryl with all my heart, I loved Jesus more, and the calling of God was strong in my heart.

I was made to think that I needed to find someone who wanted to preach. I broke up with Darryl shortly after. It broke my heart for about one year. I also knew I broke his heart as well. I thought he was God's plan for my life; it was a terrible battle of breaking up with someone I really cared deeply for.

For the record: Darryl went on to become a powerful Green Beret and did serve on a Special Forces team. He is a great father of four beautiful children. He was called into service in Iraq four times during the war. Darryl is another great man of God and is still a great friend today. I will always love and respect this man. He loves Jesus, and has done what he was called to do for Him. He's like David's "mighty men of valor."

෴෴෴෴෴෴෴෴෴෴෴෴෴෴෴෴෴෴෴෴෴෴෴

I didn't see anyone else I wanted to date, although I met nice godly men. Again, I kept myself busy in Jesus, sharing my story as God opened up more and more doors to share about His love and grace over my life.

The church was now growing, and almost a thousand people were coming in. I helped out in all different ministries: standing at the door as a greeter, driving the church van to pick up people, choir, a Christian band, outreaches, Morning Prayer- and I was still running the women's home. I'd been a Christian for ten years, and still this fire in my heart to preach burned. When the Bible conferences came, I would stand to answer every altar call: "SEND ME LORD, I'LL GO!"

I found books, and was surprised to read about women like Aimee Semple McPherson, Kathryn Kuhlman, Maria Woodworth Etter, and hundreds of women missionaries sent to preach the gospel of Jesus Christ in Africa, China, Philippines, and the Middle East. The next time my pastor came in for his haircut, I brought up the "woman" subject again. I shared with him all the books I had found, and the great things these women did for Jesus. He looked at me as if he didn't know or care. Then he said, "Every woman I know who preaches goes *crazy.*"

"What about Marilyn Hickey?" I said, "I found all these great women who preach God's Word."

He looked at me and said something *very* rude and derogatory against Pastor Hickey, not worth repeating. I was shocked: "THAT'S NOT VERY NICE!"

He just smiled, as I was finishing up. Again, as he got ready to leave, he said, "Women can't preach." Then: "Why don't you find yourself a husband?"

"I don't see anyone I want to date."

"You want to preach, find a husband who wants to preach." He parted with these words, "Then you can be a pastor's wife."

꙰ꙶ

I went home and read, over and over again, the two scriptures which are always quoted to keep women from preaching. It sure did look straightforward, but something in my spirit was churning inside. *Something wasn't right- **but what was it?"** My heart's cry was, "Jesus, help me understand!

GOD'S PLAN OR MAN'S PLAN

10

Genesis 16:3: *"Then Sarai, Abram's wife, took Hagar her maid, the Egyptian, and gave her to her husband Abram to be his wife, after Abram had dwelt ten years in the land of Canaan."*

This next chapter is very important, and yet very hard to write, as I do not want to promote rebellion in any way, shape, or form. In order for you to understand the purpose of this book, I must explain:

I had never been raised in church, so when I received Jesus as my Savior, I followed all the rules spoken to me. I never had a father, so I really looked up to my pastor as a spiritual father. I respected everything he said, and his words had authority as if they were carved in stone. Because of my great love for Jesus, I devoted my whole heart to serving Him; I wanted to comply and do what was asked of me.

I've held this story in my heart for many years, and knew that one day it must come out, in order to help others not get caught in the same trap. *As I continue to write this book, I want you to know that I have been saved now, for 35 years, but please allow me to go back, now, and continue to share what happened...*

I'd been saved for 12 years. I studied my Bible fervently, and loved Jesus with all my heart! I hadn't met anyone else I wanted to date seriously. But, I continued to have this overwhelming desire to go preach, more and more. Again conference time came, and like the previous conferences, to the altar I went, standing and praying, "*Send me, Lord, I'll go!*"

After all this time, I was still asking, "What do I need to do, if I desire to go preach? Do I go to Bible school? **What do I do?**"

I prayed, fasted, and asked, over and over again. I was doing all I could do, right where I was. I'd even started a Bible study at my workplace, midweek during the day. Three women's homes were filling up the church, and one men's home was growing strong as well. Outreaches and Bible studies were held in the women's home once a week. Also, I was still "sneak" preaching out in different places.

Once again, I asked my pastor, "*Please,* what do I do to go preach?" I asked as kindly as I could, "You send out men and they come back hurting and broken. Maybe they were not called to go out to preach. I *know* I'm called to preach, send me!"

He replied, with a stern voice: "If you want to *preach*, find a *husband!*"

"But I read where Paul said it's better to be single to do the work of God; why do I need to find a husband?"

"Because you're a woman! Find a husband; you want to preach? FIND A HUSBAND!"

"That's not fair. Send me to Africa then; lots of single women go as missionaries to other countries."

He just looked at me…

That day when the pastor left my shop I wept with all my heart. I cried out, "*Lord,* why did you make me a woman, and place this call in my heart if I can't go? I don't understand!" Every day at morning at prayer I cried out, "Use me, Lord! I know You didn't save me and bring me out of all that *junk* of the world to have me hide it. *Help me, Lord!*"

One day I met a young man, and shared Jesus with him. To my surprise he came to church, and locked in right away. I bought him a Bible and showed him where to start reading. As I walked him through the Bible, he asked me a million questions; I answered as many as I could.

It wasn't long before I realized he had a crush on me. He asked me out for coffee and I accepted. Later, he asked me out again, and before long we were hanging out. He was a good guy, and had a good job. When he asked me to date him seriously, I told him I must talk with him first. We went out to dinner and I said, "*OK,* before I say yes, I have to tell you something: I'm called to preach; do you have a problem with that?"

He smiled and said, "*No,* should I?"

"I'm a woman! I want to preach the ggospel and pioneer a church someday."

He made light of it, and replied, "Great."

We dated for almost a year before he asked the question, "Will you marry me?" It was a little harder this time, saying yes, because I felt like I would be getting married for the wrong reason: because I wanted to preach, and it seemed like it didn't bother him at all. I said, "Yes," though, and a date was set.

I didn't love this man like I should have, and felt like once again, I was *forced* into a position- the same as when I was 15 years of age. But I figured, "We both love Jesus, so with Jesus, this relationship could work." I told my pastor, "I found someone who wants to preach one day, and he knows I want to preach. I'm going to get married."

He smiled and said, "*Good* for you."

The night before the wedding, I remember sitting in my shop with my best friend Jill. I started weeping- a cry that came from deep within. She looked at me, and asked, "Are you okay?"

I sat on the chair weeping like a baby, knowing that I was getting married for all the wrong reasons. How could I tell her that I was getting married so I could go preach? I felt the Holy Spirit trying to stop me; this heaviness in my heart was not normal. I'd figured this marriage could work. I was established; I already owned my home and business. I was self-employed, had money in the bank. Sam and Kaweah were almost grown; it wouldn't be too long before they would be out of the house.

The next day, we were married, and then flew into Germany for our honeymoon. That first night, sorry to say, was a nightmare! I don't want to go into all the details of what happened. The trust and respect that a marriage is to be built on, *crumbled to pieces* that first night. I remember walking for hours and hours, day after day, in Germany.

After we returned home, I went directly to my pastor's house. I told him what had happened; that I'd made a mistake in marrying this man, and that I wanted this marriage annulled. I wept, screamed, and cried with all my heart that night in my pastor's house. He looked at me after I finished telling him everything. He told me to look at him, and said, "I know how you feel! The same thing happened with my wife on our wedding night. You're going to make it through this, I promise. We did."

I wept and cried like a baby for hours at my pastor's house that night. He prayed for me, told me to go home. Honestly, I didn't want to go home; I didn't want to go *near* my home. I wanted to run away. I'd saved myself for 13 years- "For *what?*" I thought, "Only to be hurt and broken again!"

It took me about six months to work through this violation. The only reason I made it through, was because I was a prayer warrior; no way could I let go of my prayer life! This wasn't an easy time at all; I was even a little mad at God, and I knew that I needed to forgive. I came to a decision to make this work, and that forgiveness was the only way to bring healing to this new marriage.

*Ӻ*ҿ

Time passed. Little by little, things were healing up. About a year later, my husband was told that in order for him to go higher in his position at work, he had to get his Master's Degree. His degree would be paid for, but he must choose a city from one of three locations: Turkey, Colorado, or Oregon. I knew this was an open door to preach, and was thrilled inside!

We talked about all three locations; I reminded him that I wanted to preach while he was getting his Master's Degree. We discussed each place, and I suggested we should not select Turkey, for two reasons: 1) I'm a woman and it's mostly Muslim; 2) since I'm a **bold** woman, they might kill me.

Any city in Colorado was too close to Colorado Springs, and I wanted to pioneer a church in an area that was "less" churched (I'd discovered that only 2% of the people go to church in Oregon-needless to say, that fired me up!) Not to mention, I heard that Oregon has one of the most breath-taking coastlines in all of the U.S. I dabble with paints, and imagined the joy of sitting down with my easel and making some attempts at capturing beautiful scenery on canvas. SO............

We decided on Oregon; in no time we were packed and on our way to another state. Before we left Colorado, I told my pastor, "I'm going to pioneer, start a church."

He looked at me, and said, "Well, I'm not going to give you any money to start a church."

I was so happy, I didn't even think about what he said. At last, I was going to GO PREACH! My reply to him was, "Don't worry! If it's God's will, He will supply. If it's not God, I'm not going to worry about it, but I'm not asking for any money. I'm excited!"

ℐℯ

Once we'd arrived in Oregon, I knew that it was very important to get our house in order first. We found and rented a house on top of a hill; from it we could watch as a gorgeous panoramic view of the countryside revealed itself. Moving always puts extra strain on a home, so I worked very hard unpacking and getting everything put away. Finally, our home was in order-*whew!* -now I had the house to myself all day long, as everyone was now situated in school.

I'm an early bird; I decided to pray for three hours early in the morning before I started my day. I didn't want to waste any time. After cleaning the house, and throwing something for dinner into the Crockpot, I set out to get familiar with my new town. Driving around and learning the area would help me to know what to pray for. When I noticed all the little "Darwin" tags on the bumper of cars, I was really stirred! The God I know was able to tear down that stronghold, so into prayer I went. After a few months of nothing but prayer, I decided it was time; I talked with the kids and they were excited about starting a church. I decided to start a home Bible study first, and in time we would find another location.

And that's what I did; I started a Bible study, and within less than three months it started to really grow. Before I knew it we had over 25 people! The house was getting a little crowded. After prayer one morning, I spoke with my husband and said, "I'm going to look for a building to hold services in town. If we have the church services in town, we can grow more."

Everyone was happy; the kids were doing great, and adjusted well in school. My husband had his hands full; with college and engineering homework besides, he was quite busy. I felt so complete, like I'd died and gone to heaven. Starting a church was wonderful; so many new people were coming in and getting saved. We moved our home church to the school to make room for more growth. That's just what happened; we started to have about 100 people in less than 6 months.

It was time for a Bible conference to be held in Colorado Springs. I explained the purpose of the conference with the new baby Christians, and asked, "Who would like to go back to Colorado Springs with me for a Bible conference?"

About 25 people lifted their hands. I heard them shout, "Pastor Luauna, I want to go, I want to *GO!*"

I smiled... I was so proud of each and every one of them. Our van, which held 15 people, and a few cars caravanned as we headed back for the Pastors' Conference. We made plans for housing, and everyone had a place to stay. My husband couldn't go back with us because he was in the middle of finals.

We finally arrived; I cannot tell you how I felt, and how eager to share with my pastor all the wonderful things God was doing in Oregon. Everyone else was just as excited. People were coming in from everywhere, like every other conference- only *this* time, *I* was a part of coming back to my home church to give a good report! High spirits filled the air; all our people arrived at church early, and found front row seats. They were smiling from ear to ear, and again I was so proud of them all.

At every conference, a few pastors were called on to testify what God was doing in their different cities. I was told, "Luauna, they want you to share tomorrow night." ... WOW! I wanted to jump with excitement, thinking to myself, "Wait until they see all the amazing people Jesus has touched from Oregon!"

The next night came, and everyone at the conference was filled with joy and anticipation. The pastors who'd been asked to give their report were to come up early to sit up on the platform before the service started; we all would come out from the room in back. As I was getting ready to head for the platform, my pastor walked up to me and said, "Now listen to me, Luauna; don't you say you are the pastor, do you hear me? You give your husband honor tonight. You tell them you're giving the report because your husband couldn't come."

I looked at him. I felt my heart sink to the ground as I said, "But, I'm their pastor; they've known me as their pastor for almost a year now."

He looked at me and said, "I don't care- DON'T TELL those people you're the pastor; do you understand?"

"Yes, Sir," I nodded.

He opened the door, and led me to the main platform; all the other pastors were sitting down by now. Looking around, I noticed I was the only woman sitting on the platform. My heart felt heavy, but as I looked around and saw all those people, I bowed my head to say a little prayer, "Father, forgive me! I don't want to be angry; maybe it's my pride for feeling like I do right now, I'm so sorry. It's not about me anyway; it's all about You! Cover me, Father, in the blood of Jesus, and help me give a great report tonight. Amen."

The praise started, and I stood and praised with all my heart. I needed this heaviness lifted from me before I gave a report. One pastor after another stood up and gave a report. Then my name was called. As I stood up it was funny- all the people I brought stood up and cheered, *"Yeah, Pastor Luauna!"* I thought to myself, "Shhhhh!" but I just smiled; they were new Christians, so innocent in heart, and excited about the conference.

I never told anyone what my pastor had told me that night before I went out to the platform. That night I said, "My husband and I pastor in Oregon, and he couldn't be here." But I did give a good report sharing about all the people who were saved, and what God was doing in a state where many said, *"No one* goes to church!"

♪❀

When we returned back to Oregon, I still said nothing. Did it really matter? *No!* Not really. After all, people were getting saved and filled with the Holy Spirit; that was our purpose anyway. The church continued to grow steadily, and I *loved* every bit of it. Even though we had to break down for every service and pack up all the equipment, it didn't matter. Everyone was helping, and things were great.

After a while, I decided to start praying for our own building, so we could do more. We needed a base, a church building of our own. In Oregon, for almost a year now, the church was really starting to grow strong and people were being filled with the Holy Spirit every service. A few days each week I would hit the streets with a team, pass out flyers, and tell everyone I met about Jesus.

"This is our place forever- *Oregon!*" I would say, "This is *God's Land!*"

One day, while driving on a main road, I saw *it*- THE building! It was perfect. I pulled over and saw that it was for sale. I drove into the parking lot, walked up and looked into the window. I thought to myself, "This looks like it used to be a church."

As my heart skipped a beat, I *knew:* this was it!

I laid hands on the building right there in the parking lot and prayed, "I CLAIM THIS BUILDING for the GLORY of the Lord, in JESUS' name!" I wrote down the number, made the call, and set an appointment to talk about the building.

I sat down with the family at dinner that night and told them, "I think I found a building; it would be our own building, our own church." Everyone was filled with as much excitement as I was. When we went to see it, I was ecstatic about what we found: the church came with a small house, and it had another building, which was perfect for an office. It was on a main street corner, which gave good visibility and easy access for everyone to come to church. It wasn't long before I'd signed papers to purchase the building, leased with an option to buy. We had a few years to build up funds, and in time it would be our building completely.

I felt like everything was falling into place. I didn't even think about the violation on our wedding night; it didn't matter anymore. I had forgiven him, and wanted to have a good example of a Christian marriage for the people at church. I made sure my house was always picked up and clean, and made dinner almost every night so we could all eat together; this was very important to me. I always thought to myself, "If a family eats together, prays together- it stays together." My husband and kids were busy with school, and I kept myself busy with my garden, keeping my home in order, church, prayer, and studying for the next sermon.

I knew we needed to move from the parsonage of the church we were living in, to turn it into a women's home. A woman in the church was selling her home, an old log cabin. It came with five acres, and a year-around creek. I loved it! and knew that with a little TLC (Tender Loving Care), it would be perfect for church campouts and maybe even a place for prayer. I worked hard; we saved money and bought the cabin.

It wasn't long before the women's home was filled with 15 women.

In the back of the office building, there was plenty of room to start a men's home as well. That's just what I did; it was filled and we had over 18 men. I worked hard every day and started training leaders for home cell groups. Both my kids were involved, and a great part of growing the work for Jesus. Sam played drums; Kaweah sang and helped lead worship; she also started a youth group.

Our worship team was *amazing!* A man named Dave, from a top music store, got saved, and played excellent lead guitar and drums; he was such a blessing. His wife, Gail, jumped right in, and became a wonderful help. In time we had five vocalists, lead and rhythm guitars, bass player, keyboard & piano, trumpet, saxophone, and congas. We were shaking heaven with praise, and it was awesome!

Two years went by fast, and we were running over 200 people. Everything was great; monies came in to cover all the needs of both the men's and women's homes and all the church expenses. The people were so faithful in paying their tithes, and there was such a wonderful presence of the Holy Spirit. I decided maybe it was time for my pastor to come to Oregon to see firsthand what God was doing. I talked to my husband and shared with our church; all were excited and eager for him to visit. I called and asked my pastor to please come and preach a three-day meeting. I explained to him that I wanted him to see everything that the Lord was doing in Oregon, and that I would take care of his airfare, hotel, and of course, he'd receive a great honorarium.

We worked hard to get everything ready for the meeting; we passed out flyers, prepared the grounds, and cleaned up the church building. Everything was in order. Anticipation was in the air; the men's and women's homes were thrilled. The day for the meeting came. The first night was packed. *What fun!* We began with a powerful praise and worship service; everyone lifting up his or her hands, singing praise and the Holy Spirit flowing through the service, was incredible. The second night carried with it a sense of increasing exhilaration. The third night was standing room only; our ushers worked hard to find chairs for everyone, and we even had some of the kids sit in the front row on the floor in order to make room for everyone. Words of prophecy flowed, with praise; some of the new people were saved, filled with the Holy Spirit, and the Master's hand was in His house to bring healing to many.

I was so pleased after the service, walking outside in to the parking lot with my pastor, along with my friend Jill. I was smiling from ear to ear. I stopped and asked, "Well, what do you think?"

He just looked at me; I thought maybe he didn't understand my question.

I stood smiling like a little kid, waiting for his approval: "Tell me, isn't God great? He's doing such an amazing work." I stood excited, waiting, "Well, tell me! What do you think?"

He looked at me, rolled up his sleeve, looked at his watch, and then said, "It's getting late."

I was taken aback by his response; I looked at Jill and then back at my pastor. "Well, tell me what you think about the church?"

Again, just looking at me, then his watch: "It's getting late, take me to my hotel."

I was shocked; I stood there looking at him; I wanted to cry. And then I asked, "Can't you just once say you believe in me?"

He looked at me again and said, "I told you before, I don't believe in women preachers. It's getting late; please take me to my hotel. I have an early flight tomorrow."

Jill went with me that night to drive him to his hotel; we all were silent in the car. On the drive back to the church Jill asked me, "Are you okay?"

I said, "Sure," but I really wanted to cry, I felt so rejected. I realized that night there was nothing I could do to prove I had a call of God on my life.

I felt defeated, and I hurt inside. I lived about 15 minutes from the church; as I drove home that night alone, I prayed and wept. How could I have felt so much victory, and now such heaviness? I prayed all the way home, and never said anything to my kids. I never wanted to put a sour taste for ministry in any way, shape, or form in their hearts. I hid all these feelings and emotions inside. I didn't even share them with my husband, because he was still pretty young in the Lord, and I didn't want to shake him up in any way, to cause him to stumble in his walk.

Maybe from having the women's home, I had learned to be very careful with what I would say- anything negative could cause someone to stumble or fall away. Since I'd read Dr. Dobson's books, I learned also to never speak negative about church to your children; it could cause them to become resentful towards church or church people when they are older. I found myself protecting them, and dealt with problems in the church right on the spot. But as for my family, I was like a mother hen who protects her chicks; protecting them was part of pastoring a church.

The meetings were now over, and we were back to building the Kingdom of God. I was planning and preparing for the vision of what I felt the Holy Spirit wanted for the church. My husband and Kaweah were back in school, and I was back to studying for my sermons, spending time in prayer, and helping the women's and men's homes grown in Jesus. By this time my son had met someone, and they were married.

Months had passed since the meeting. I was noticing something different in my husband. Tension was starting to grow between us; it was becoming obvious that he was not happy at all. I figured it was from all the pressure of college. I asked him, "What's going on?"

It was hard to know how he couldn't be happy; we had everything we needed, or so I thought. We had a home, a great church, and the ministry was growing and doing great. I thought I'd died and gone to heaven; I was doing just what I wanted to do, and I loved every moment of it.

It was getting close to graduation, and my husband would have to give back a few years to his work, because they'd paid for his Master's Degree. He told me it was only a matter of time, and we were going to have to leave for a year or two. I thought, "No problem. We'll bring in someone to help us so when we return we can continue to build the church." I was still excited, because I figured Oregon was where God wanted us to plant our roots.

The tension between my husband and I continued to escalate; I didn't know what was going on. Suddenly, he became bitter towards me. When I would preach, on the drive home right after church, he would say, "If it was me, I wouldn't have preached that message." More and more, he said things, trying to put me down.

One day I asked, "Are you mad at me? Why are you being so negative about my preaching?" Little by little, I could feel his pride rise up, and it caused continual strife. He started speaking more and more negative words.

I wouldn't have minded his help- constructive criticism is never bad, if it is given with the right heart. He'd only been saved for maybe three years, and I knew he had some growing to do. I could see and feel a change in our relationship, and became very concerned. After a while, we couldn't even communicate. Everything I did, somehow, was wrong. I couldn't get a grasp of where this was coming from. I spent a lot of time in prayer, and a lot of time at church.

One day he said something that cut to the very core of my heart: "Maybe you shouldn't be preaching, because you're a woman!"

His words were like a razor to my heart. I hadn't told him all I'd gone through in my past.

I stood there, looking at him, and said to him that day, "I don't know what's going on, but don't make me choose between you and God, because if you do, you'll lose."

I reminded him, how I'd told him before we were married; "I told you I wanted to preach the Gospel of Jesus Christ. I told you I was going to pioneer a church for Jesus. Where is all this coming from?"

Nothing more was said, but the tension grew between us.

THE TRUTH UNFOLDS

11

Psalm 31:4-5; "Pull me out of the net which they have secretly laid for me, for You are my strength. Into Your hand I commit my spirit; You have redeemed me, O Lord God of truth."

Months passed and the time was winding down; we would have to travel out of the country for about a year, possibly two. We were going to go into Seoul, Korea. I was pretty excited inside, because I had heard and read about the largest Spirit-filled Christian church in the world, which was located in Seoul.

I knew I had to pick a couple to care for and uphold the church while we were gone, because everyone in our church was very young in the Lord; they were baby Christians.

I decided to call my pastor in Colorado and let him know that we had to go to Korea. I shared with him that we needed a couple whom we could trust to come in for a year or two, to help work with the church, minister, and continue building the work until we returned from Korea.

He suggested a few names, but those he mentioned, I felt, were not right for this work. We continued to pray; there was little time, but it was winding down before we needed to depart.

A week later, I got a call from my pastor. He said, "I have the perfect couple. They've come in from China and only want to be stateside for one or two years. Then they would need to return back to China."

I said, "Sounds perfect!" Everything was set up; they came in, and I shared everything with them. We spent some time together, I introduced them to the congregation, and there was a good feeling all around. It seemed like a perfect fit. I knew a year or two would go by fast, and we would return to something great.

Faster than you can shake a stick, we were packed and on our way to Seoul, South Korea. Sam was married; he and his wife went to live in Arizona, so that left us three going to Korea.

I was stirred up inside, and couldn't wait. I had heard so much about this man of God, Dr. David Yonggi Cho, and now, we'd get a chance to meet him, and see his church. As soon as we arrived in Seoul, Korea, it was instant culture shock. Cars were everywhere; three lanes were like five. Everything was completely different; I knew it would take a little bit of time to get settled in.

But I was excited at the same time- all those people- where *did* they come from? Even late at night the streets were packed; it seemed like the city never slept. The population was almost 20 million. Our first week was spent in a major hotel, which was beautiful. Everywhere I turned I saw all the signs were in Korean writing, and I wondered how long it would take me to learn what some of those signs meant. We were jetlagged and needed to sleep, but knew it was very important that we not sleep during the day, or we would have our nights and days mixed up.

After a few days our bodies seemed to settle down, and had adjusted to the time. We still did not have housing, but at least we were adapting. I decided to go outside the hotel and look around. As I stood at the top of the stairs of the hotel, I noticed a gold-colored Mercedes-Benz parked right in front. A lady in her dress suit with a nice bag in her hand walked right up to me. She smiled and asked if I was new to Korea; her English shocked me, as it was quite good. When I told her that she spoke English well, she replied, "I practice every day so I can speak to Americans. I want to tell them about Jesus." Then she started to tell me all about Jesus; I didn't have the heart to tell her I was already a preacher. I let her continue on, and just grinned at her. The next day was Sunday, and she asked me, "Are you going to church tomorrow?"

I told her, "I don't know many churches yet." she smiled and said, "Good! Then tomorrow I will pick you up and you will visit my church."

I asked her what church she went to, and she answered, "Yoido Full Gospel Church. Have you heard of my pastor, his name is Dr. Yonggi Cho?"

I knew, right away! This was God's plan, a divine appointment. When I told her, "I would love to go to your church," she was so happy.

The following morning, she picked me up; Kaweah and I were ready for church. My husband did not go with me the first day, as he had something he had to complete. Before we drove off, this young woman placed both of her hands on the steering wheel, bowed her head and prayed. It wasn't long before I figured out why she prayed. The driving was crazy; you are completely under God's grace there!

When we arrived, I didn't see the church anywhere; I didn't realize we'd parked five blocks away. Men were ushering the cars from five blocks away; with cheerful faces, they were helping everyone to find a parking place.

We jumped out of the car, and she walked quickly, with us in tow. As we got closer I couldn't believe this massive building, but what was astounding were the thousands of people. People were everywhere; like a herd of cattle side-by-side, we flowed into the church. And within 15 minutes, thousands and thousands of people were seated, worshipping, and praying, even before the service was to begin. We were on the third floor; as I looked over the banister I was in awe. I couldn't believe this vast crowd. What amazed me more was that each person sat down in their seat; they prayed and prayed, and prayed. This was before the service started; no one talked to anyone, but they all prayed in the spirit before church service.

Then all of a sudden, the orchestra musicians started the old gospel hymns, playing them to perfection. As I looked around, everyone had joined in, clapping and singing with all their hearts. The power of God's presence was strong; I was clapping right along beside them, and so was Kaweah. The lady who brought us sat in a different area- she'd said that our section was for those who spoke English - after church she would come back to get me. I looked around and noticed other English-speaking people. I was amazed at what I saw! I couldn't believe all these people in one place, filled with the Holy Spirit, filled with victory, praying with their whole hearts; it was GLORIOUS!

After the service, the young lady who'd brought us to the church service came back, with a smile on her face as she asked me, "How did you like the service?"

I replied, "I loved it!"

I could tell that we'd made her day. She said, "Let me show you around the big church."

As we were walking, another Korean woman walked up to us. Her name was Pastor Lee Hae Kyu. She too smiled and spoke perfect English, as she asked me, "Where are you from?" I explained to her that I was from Colorado, but living now in

Oregon, where I pioneered a church. She was delighted; she turned and asked the woman who'd brought us, "Please allow me to show her the big church, so I can practice my English." I smiled, and Pastor Lee said, "Come, let's go; she will come back in one hour."

Talk about a divine appointment! You know it's God's divine appointment when you meet Dr. Cho's personal English interpreter in the midst of 25,000 people. She and I became great friends from that first day. Within a month we partnered together and were preaching through South Korea. She was a treasure, and a gift to me personally.

In time she took me up to Dr. Cho's office, and introduced me to everyone, including Dr. Cho's personal secretary. Lydia was her name; she also became a great friend of mine. She was a widow, an American white woman who had spent over 30 years in Korea as a missionary preaching the gospel with her husband before he died. Dr. Cho, knowing this woman's worth, brought her into the big church and took care of her. She was now in charge of all contacts calling from USA. Her husband had been a great friend to Dr. Cho; for many years they had preached together before he became sick and went to be with the Lord.

ᘓᎫ

I had been in Korea now for four months, and I am not one for dreams. Our house was all set up and everything seemed to be in order. But one night I was awakened, shaking, by a strange dream. I sat up in bed; my heart was beating like it was going to pop out of my chest. I was so disturbed that I stayed awake for about one hour, thinking about the dream.

The next morning, I said nothing about the dream to anyone, but I started a fast. I decided if there was a meaning behind this dream, I needed to hear from God. I fasted on water. I hadn't set up any meetings for the next seven days, so I decided that I would spend all day in prayer and fasting. Something was happening inside; I was so troubled, all I could do was pray in the Spirit. On the sixth day of fasting on only water, I felt the Holy Spirit speak to my heart, "Check on the church back home."

I thought to myself, "How is that possible? I'm in Korea clear on the other side of the world." I prayed to the Lord, "If You want me to check on the church back home then You must show me- open a door back to the United States, and I will know it is You."

The next day, I received a call from the US, from a woman out of LA. She asked me, "Is this Pastor Luauna?"

I answered, "Yes."

"I heard you speak a while back in Arizona. Would you please come and be one of our main speakers, along with Bill Wilson out of New York, for our Bible conference?"

I knew right then, God was opening the door. This was truly God's way of getting me to go back and check on the church. I asked her, "Would you mind if I bought the ticket from this side, so I can check on my church, and then I would drive to LA for the meeting?"

She said, "Yes, I will reimburse you for any of your costs, and pay for your gas to LA."

I called and made reservations, but I didn't call the church back home; I was going to surprise them. I was happy to be going back for a visit, even though I had only been gone four months.

When I arrived at the airport in Portland, Oregon, I had someone meet me with my car. I'd told them not to let anyone know that I was coming back, so I could surprise everyone...

Well, the surprise was **mine!** As I drove up to the church, a U-Haul truck was backed up to the door; they were packing all the equipment inside the truck. As I walked across the parking lot, the man I had asked to come and help build the church was now walking towards me.

He was as nervous as a cat on a hot tin roof, and I was still fasting on water. When he looked at me, I saw a different look on his face. I looked at the U-Haul, and then looked at him. He then lifted up his voice, and asked me, "What are *you* doing here?"

I looked at him; the tone of his voice threw me off guard.

"What are you doing?" I asked, "What is the U-Haul doing here?"

He answered, "You're not supposed to be here!"

I was puzzled; I didn't understand anything he was saying. I looked at him, and asked again, "What are you doing?"

He said, "We're moving!"

"Moving?" I was still puzzled, naïve, stupid- I still couldn't understand what he was saying. "Were you going to tell anyone you were moving? What about the people?"

He must've thought I was so dumb. I was shocked at his answer, "They're coming with us!"

Have you ever had such a sick feeling in the pit of your stomach?

He turned around to motion for the U-Haul to leave. I stood there in shock; I had no understanding what was going on. Then he said, "You're not welcome here."

I just looked at him, "What do you mean I'm not welcome here? This is my church!"

"Not anymore! No one is behind you, not even your pastor. Wake up!"

I said, "What are you talking about?"

Just standing there, he replied, "Ask the pastor!"

He gave me the keys, then turned around, walked off to his car, and drove away. I stood in the parking lot, watching as he left. Wondering in my mind, "What is going on?" I walked into the office, picked up the phone to call my pastor in Colorado. I left a message with his secretary for him to please call me, but no one called back.

I thought to myself, "What about all the people? What about the church? What am I going to do? I have to be in LA in two days, and then I'm scheduled to go back to Korea."

I called a woman from the church to meet with me. I discovered that this couple had undermined the entire work; they spoke spiritual death into the hearts of every single one of these new converts. They'd told them I was a woman; that I had no business preaching, and that no one was behind me.

Right in to middle of all this I knew I still needed to go to LA, as I was already scheduled. I preached for three days, then came back to Oregon and tried to call my pastor in Colorado. Again, I received no call back. I still had those three women's homes in Colorado going strong, so I called my good friend Jill, who'd been left in charge of them, and told her I was coming to Colorado.

I didn't tell her what was going on; I told her I needed to see the pastor, and that I'd be there for a few days. She was happy of course, but she knew nothing. I flew into Colorado, and called again leaving a message with my pastor's secretary, "I'm in Colorado. I need to meet with my pastor." Again, no return calls. For nine days, I would call, over and over. Finally, on the tenth day I jumped into my car and drove to the church. I figured I could catch them in the morning. I walked inside and waited, and after a while, my pastor walked in through the door. He looked up; we made eye contact, and I said, "I have been trying to call you for days; I need to talk to you." I could tell he was nervous.

He pulled a lollipop out of his pocket, took the wrapper off, and put it in his mouth. Then he turned around; there was another pastor standing on the side, and he called to him, "Jack- come up with me to my office." Then he turned around, glanced at me, and said, "Come on up." As I sat down on a chair in his office across from his desk, I looked at him. I was still fasting. "What's going on?" I told him, "They split the church; they told me to ask you why? Do you want to tell me what's going on?"

He gave me an icy stare, and replied scornfully, "I told you; I don't believe in women preachers."

I was stunned, to say the least; I couldn't believe what I'd just heard. I looked at him, and said, "Over 200 converts, 200 *new* converts- does anyone care about *them?* Why would somebody do such a thing? They're innocent; they're in the middle of all this. I was in Korea! Why? How could somebody do such a thing?"

I felt the tears well up in me, and then all of a sudden he looked at me, and said, "Stop your crying; *that's* why we don't have women in ministry."

I wasn't crying to cry, I was angry. I felt the anger of the Lord. Then he glanced up at the other pastor across from him and said, "Isn't that right Jack, women aren't supposed to preach, are they?"

This man looked over at me, and I felt the tears were starting to fall down my cheeks. He answered, "Yeah! You're right, because if she were a man, we'd just jack him up against a wall and tell him, 'Stop your crying!'"

They both snickered, and grinned at each other. I looked at Jack, and said, "Yeah right! That's just what Jesus would do- RIGHT, Jack- His disciples up against a wall?" Jack looked at me and started to say something more, but I stopped him right in his tracks:

"Stop! You're not my pastor, and you never have been, and by the way, you don't even like people." I knew him, and I knew how he treated people, including his wife

I looked at my pastor, and stood up with tears falling out of my eyes, making a puddle right on top of his desk. I leaned over, and told him, "I served you for 13 years faithfully. I loved you. I respected you. I gave my all. I have been faithful. I have loved Jesus with all my heart, from the day I was saved. I have done nothing wrong! GUILTY! YES, I'm guilty- guilty of **one** thing- loving people and preaching the gospel. I cannot believe you allowed such an evil thing to happen to over 200 people, baby Christians; did anyone think about *them?* Did anyone *care* about them?"

I stood with both hands on top of his desk, weeping, and barely catching my breath as I spoke, I was so broken. Looking down at him I continued, "I loved you as a father, a father I never had. I served this church in ministry with all my heart, mind, and soul. I gave my all. I gave my best. I gave everything. Nothing was good enough; no matter what I did, I couldn't meet your standards. **Nothing!** Not one thing I did was good enough all these years, 13 years."

Then I bowed my head and prayed out loud, right on the spot. "Lord, I forgive this man, I forgive him. Help me *Jesus.* Help the new converts.   Jesus, I place this man in the palm of Your hands."

I then looked at him, tears running down my face like a faucet opened full force, as I said, "I'm sorry I can't be a part of this anymore. I need to cut the strings today. I do forgive you! But, I need to say *good-bye.*"

I turned and walked out the door, down the stairs, and into my car. That day I drove to the mountains and wept like a little baby.

-- AND UNFOLDS

12

Luke 12:2-3; "For there is nothing covered that will not be revealed, nor hidden that will not be known. Therefore whatever you have spoken in the dark will be heard in the light, and what you have spoken in the ear in inner rooms will be proclaimed on the housetops."

I sat in the mountains in Colorado for what seemed like hours weeping that day, crying out to the Lord. I felt so alone and forsaken. My heart hurt, as if someone had ripped it out of my chest, thrown it on the ground, and stomped all over it. I could barely breathe through all the crying.

I knew I had to get ahold of my emotions. But what was I going to do? I couldn't even tell my best friend Jill what was happening. She knew nothing. I felt so confused at that very moment. I'd catch my breath just for a minute, and then start to weep all over again. I couldn't talk to anyone, because I didn't want to shake up anyone's spiritual foundation. After a few hours of crying, I couldn't even cry anymore, I was so worn out.

My return ticket back to Oregon was scheduled for the next day. I drove back to the women's home and was very thankful that no one was there. I took a shower, redid my makeup and tried to look presentable. When Jill came home from work that evening, I kept back from her what had happened. She was still running my three women's homes in Colorado Springs, and I owned the main home. Jill knew something was wrong; she asked me if I was okay. I lifted my hand, half smiled and motioned; "Please don't ask me that question right now. I don't want to talk about it." She said, "Okay, then let's go get something to eat."

The next day Jill took me to the airport. I still wasn't sure what I was going to do. I arrived in Portland, and the drive was over an hour to my house. I had a million thoughts running through my head, it seemed- all at the same time. That first night back, I finally fell asleep. The next day I went to church to look around. As I was walking through the church, I remembered the joy of all the people, as each one was saved. In through the door came Jennifer; she was one of the first young girls who'd come to the church I first started in my home. I didn't think anyone was left. She looked at me, smiled, shrugged her shoulders, and said, "Now what are we gonna do?"

I felt a tear start to rise, and my chin began to quiver. This beautiful little redheaded girl walked up to me, gave me a big hug, and said, "I'm still here!" My lips curled up into a smile, and I swallowed the lump in my throat. I thought to myself, "I've got to be strong."

⌘⌘⌘⌘⌘⌘⌘⌘⌘⌘⌘⌘⌘⌘⌘⌘⌘⌘⌘⌘⌘⌘⌘⌘⌘

After several days, a few more people came back. There were about seven to ten of us. I called my husband, but didn't tell him anything about what my pastor had said, because he too was so young in Jesus. I didn't want to shake his foundation in the Lord. But I did share with him about the couple, and how they split the church and started another one 20 miles away. He asked me, "What are you going to do?"

I told him, "I don't know; I need a few days to pray." I could neither leave the building, nor could I let go of a handful of people who'd been caught in the middle of all this confusion, and were just hanging. I felt as if I was stuck between a rock and a hard place. My daughter Kaweah was in Korea attending high school, in 11th grade. My son and his wife were still in Arizona, and I was supposed to be in Korea.

I looked at the handful of people left behind and thought, "This is truly a test!"

I couldn't blame the young people who'd left; they were still new converts, young babies in Jesus. What could I do now? I thought I knew this couple! I thought my pastor loved me. I can't begin to tell you what I felt inside, because there aren't any words one can find to express, to share the great anguish this betrayal caused.

After a few days of prayer, I decided I would stay back in Oregon and try to rebuild the church. I couldn't just leave the building; I'd signed papers to purchase the property and to abandon it or the people who were left behind was not an option.

Also, there was no way I could bring my daughter Kaweah back, in the midst of all this chaos, confusion, and strife. I felt it would be better if she stayed in Korea for a few months until things smoothed out. I wasn't about to have my son and his new wife return from Arizona in the midst of all this; I felt their marriage needed to be protected as well.

Of course, I wanted my family back home, but there was so much going on at the moment. Dealing with a church split was like trying to put the pieces back together after a Category 5 tornado lays waste an entire city. Where do you start? What's most important? All I could do was pray. Every day I found myself having to forgive the couple, but it wasn't easy.

᪑᪑᪑᪑᪑᪑᪑᪑᪑᪑᪑᪑᪑᪑᪑᪑᪑᪑᪑᪑᪑᪑᪑᪑᪑᪑

Little by little, the church started to grow again. But it wasn't growing as fast as it had been, before. There was still a lot of confusion, and a lot of unanswered questions. It was like driving through the fog at night, mixed with a blend of dark clouds. This darkness I felt was so demonic. I felt I had to wade through hell's demons, and I spent hour after hour in prayer.

First, I knew I had to forgive this couple who had split this church. I knew Satan hated the works done here. All Satan wanted was to steal, kill, and destroy the very purposes of God in this place. I thought about the verse in Genesis Chapter One when God spoke, "Let there be light." The invisible war that must have taken place when God Almighty spoke those words! The light *had* to come forth; it broke through the darkness at the very moment God's spoken Word went forth.

᪑᪑᪑᪑᪑᪑᪑᪑᪑᪑᪑᪑᪑᪑᪑᪑᪑᪑᪑᪑᪑᪑᪑᪑᪑᪑

I had studied this state, Oregon, and its history before even coming into the city. As we drove in the first thing I noticed was how every other car bumper had a Darwin emblem. It was an "Anti-God" area; this place was bound by Darwinism, the occult, and witchcraft. Not many people attended church, and many of those who did go were not filled with the Holy Spirit. Church was like a social club for many- not all- but many. I was excited about coming into the city to bring the message of salvation: "Jesus is alive- the Word from the Lord God Almighty!"

*Coming to town, I knew the light of God dwelt within us; we are the salt of the earth. We, the Church, those who have been washed in the blood of **Jesus**, and walk in faith, are Satan's threat, and I realized the devil did not like what we were doing.*

We were breaking through the darkness, bringing forth the **light***; souls were being saved, and delivered out of darkness.*

I think we made the devil mad!

༺♫༻♫༺♫༺♫༺♫༺♫༺♫༺♫༺♫༺♫༺♫༺♫༺♫༺♫༺♫༺♫༺♫༺

Our little team started to work hard again, and gradually the church was starting to pick up the broken pieces. Healing was coming, little by little, to all of us. But it wasn't easy; I ran into people whom I loved, but their heart had been tainted against me. All I could do was pray for them, and that's exactly what I did- pray.

༺♫༻♫༺♫༺♫༺♫༺♫༺♫༺♫༺♫༺♫༺♫༺♫༺♫༺♫༺♫༺♫༺♫༺

About eight months later, my husband decided to return, along with my daughter Kaweah. She and I had never been apart; she became angry and hurt when she saw what had happened, and didn't understand any of it. She couldn't grasp the reasons people left. She asked, "I thought they loved us?"

To a young teenager, it was hard to explain, but I tried to help her to comprehend, saying, "It's not their fault; they are young in the Lord, and they were lied to."

I shared and prayed with her every day, and I reminded her how she needed to forgive everyone. I could tell she was a little distant at first; but bit-by-bit she came out of it. I was so glad she didn't come home right after the split; she would have been right in the line of fire. I'll never know for sure if it could have damaged her heart for ministry in the future; despite this experience, Kaweah has become a strong woman in the Lord today.

I kept myself busy, and slowly the church was starting to grow again. I thought everything was better, but I could still feel the tension from my husband. I knew he didn't understand everything that had happened recently, because he was a new Christian, so I didn't tell him a lot.

Maybe that was my downfall; I probably could have opened up more to him; at the time, I couldn't see bringing him into the middle of the lies and turmoil.

I still had my women's homes running in Colorado Springs, and wasn't sure what to do with them; I knew I needed to tell Jill what had happened, but I also knew that it could end our friendship forever.

A couple months before, Jill had been in a car wreck and received a small settlement. We'd always talked about going to Australia, and one day she surprised me, "You want to go with me to Australia? I'm buying the tickets."

I thought to myself, "Hallelujah!" I needed a vacation; I shared with my husband about Australia, and how much I'd like to go. Plans were made, and the date was set.

I decided to call a few people, and set up some preaching engagements while we were there. I knew that this would be the perfect time to share with Jill everything that had happened. I told her, "What I have to tell you, could end our friendship forever..."

We had been friends for over 15 years. When I explained to her that I was no longer a part of the fellowship she belonged to, she was shocked. After she'd heard it all, she was in tears; I didn't know what she was going to say. I told her about the split, having to start over at the church, and how I wanted to start another women's home in Oregon. I told her I was thinking about selling my house in Colorado. She looked at me, tears still in her eyes, and said, "You're really not coming back to Colorado, are you?"

I told her, "I don't think so." Then I changed the subject, "Let's just have fun! We are in Australia, and it's beautiful. Let's enjoy this vacation, and let's *not* talk about it anymore."

How I needed that vacation, and what a relief to share with Jill! I hadn't talked to anyone who was strong in the Lord, so I had a lot bottled up inside.

♪⁂

Jill was employed at Compassion International in Colorado Springs; two weeks after we returned home, a speaker came to visit them. The speaker came from Africa. His topic (God's timing always amazes me!) was about women! He shared how God uses women, and he began to read in the book of Genesis. Jill said, "It was like the word of God was jumping off the pages and speaking right to my heart and mind. It was revelation after revelation."

That day God spoke to Jill, and showed her that it was okay for me to preach. She called me up later that night, and said, "Wow, I believe it- you are called by God! It's okay to be a preacher; today a speaker came, and God spoke right to my heart."

Then she broke the news, "I want to move to Oregon; I want to help you. I believe God has called me to be a helper, and to help you accomplish all God wants you to do. I have the gift of helps, and I believe I'm called to help you."

I thought to myself, "How in the world is this going to work out?"

Jill went right to work; she began to mobilize all the women, moving them out of the house I owned so I could put it on the market and sell it. She asked me to pray with her; she was going to talk to the pastor, to share with him that she was moving to Oregon. I knew for a fact, that would go over like a lead balloon. But her mind was made up; she gave notice at work, put the house on the market, and in time it sold. She hadn't moved yet; she was making sure all the other girls were settled into other homes, and in the right place.

When Jill told the pastors she was moving to Oregon, they shook their heads, "No," then: "Luauna has no proven ministry."

Jill was shocked at that statement; she looked them straight in the eye, and said, "I have been friends with her for 15 years; if she doesn't have proven ministry, then there is no hope for any of us."

There was no convincing them; she told them she was sorry, but wanted to let them know that she was leaving, and wanted their blessing. They did not bless her, but said, "You are making a big mistake, and we cannot come in agreement with you."

Jill said, "I'm sorry, but I believe it's God's will for me to go to Oregon and help Pastor Luauna."

My daughter started her senior year, and by degrees things began to come back together. I started another women's home; only this time I bought a set of duplexes to house the women. I decided I needed to reach out to find another place, other pastors to fellowship with. I heard about a Bible conference; the venue was in Seattle, Washington. Pastor Casey Treat and his wife Wendy were hosting it. I was eager to go; I needed encouraging. When I arrived at their church it felt so different; the excitement was amazing, the people were ecstatic, and everyone seemed to be so friendly. There were thousands of people- I would guess almost 5,000- and pastors from all over the world at this conference. It was called, "Vision." As the conference started the praise was powerful; I felt the Holy Spirit right away. I wanted to hear from God. I needed a healing inside. I needed to know that God loved me.

I was surprised when Pastor Casey Treat's wife, Wendy, stood up to minister and she preached as well as her husband. I spent a couple of days there, and was refreshed. Pastor Casey and Wendy Treat's "Vision" Conference was like balm on a wound, and oasis in the desert that soaked into my sick heart and soothed my weary soul.

I found out about their youth conference and sent Kaweah and our teens there to get refreshed as well. Casey Treat's church was called, "Christian Faith Center." It was a Spirit-filled church; they were on fire for Jesus, and they preached the word of God. I so needed the renewal they brought to my heart and my spirit. When I sent our youth to the conference, they too came back on fire.

It seemed like everything was coming back together, except- the breach between my husband and me was increasing. I knew something was wrong, but I was so sick of all the strife, discord, and animosity I had just gone through for the 8 months while they'd been in Korea-

I WAS SICK OF FIGHTING-

So I ignored it.

When discord in a marriage is ignored, it's like having a mound of trash in your front room with a rug over it; everyone walks around it, pretending it's not there, and no one deals with the problem. My daughter was now finishing up her last year of high school, and graduation was just around the corner. I'd tried never to argue or fight in front of my kids, Sam or Kaweah; they'd not even know we were fighting. When we were about to get into an argument or something heated, I would ask my husband, "Can we talk about this outside please?" We would then go for a long walk. I had read in Dr. James Dobson's books, if you're going to fight, get out of the sight of the children. Even though my daughter was in high school, I still didn't want her to see a marriage full of strife, so I never said anything to my husband in front of her.

The pressure was getting intense though; I knew it was a matter of time before we would really start to argue back and forth. I didn't want to fight in front of my daughter. Graduation came, and Kaweah decided she wanted to go to college. I thought, "That's a great idea."

In my mind, I thought, "Maybe I could get her to move into the women's home; it is closer to town and to the college. She wouldn't be in the midst of the turmoil between my husband and me."

My daughter surprised me; she came to me, and said, "Mom, I've been thinking; I want to move out."

It was perfect timing. I smiled at her and said, "That's a good idea! How about moving inside the women's home? There's an extra room."

She asked one of her friends to move in with her, and before long she was packed, moved, and had started college.

My son was married and living on his own, and now my daughter had moved out. I thought it would be easier for us to find time to communicate, but it didn't get easier; the tension between us escalated. There was something else going on, but I couldn't put my finger on it. I decided to call a pastor couple who had been in ministry for over 35 years. I told them we needed help; we needed marriage counseling. They surprised me- the following week they were in their car, driving from LA to Oregon. We met with them, and I opened up and shared with them what was going on. (I don't want to go into all of the detail, because what my husband was involved in doesn't matter anymore.)

At that time the pastor brought correction and direction to help our relationship. He told my husband, because of what he had been involved in, it was important that he would step down for a few months, and not be involved in platform ministry. Please remember that he'd only been saved less than 5 ½ years.

After the pastor and his wife left, I thought things would get easier, but they didn't. The bickering and fighting increased, and after a few months went by we barely were talking to each other. I felt so condemned as a Christian; how could this be? What was going on? Then it all came out; he told me, "I believe women should not be preaching."

My heart sunk, I thought it would stop beating, and I was so angry. I thought to myself, "Good night! When is this all gonna stop?"

I was beginning to heal, and thought all of this stuff was over, but it was just beginning. What I didn't know was that my husband was receiving calls from my pastor back in Colorado, telling him he should be the man: "Rise up! Tell your wife to sit down!"

All of this stuff started coming to the surface, and yes, I was angry, and very hurt. Every time I preached, on the way home it would start all over again, my husband telling me, "I wouldn't preach that, or I wouldn't do that."

He continually put me down. I found myself taking long walks; we lived out in the country by all the Christmas tree farms. Sometimes I would walk for 5 miles at a time. I found a secret place to pray on one of the mountaintops. I would cry out to God, "Lord, I've served for 18 years and still *no one* believes that You called me. I'm not doing this for me; I'm preaching because You called me. Should I sit down and do nothing? It's not fair! Jesus help me!"

Again, I called Pastor Eddie; he tried to talk to my husband, telling him, "Your wife's calling is of God. She is anointed to do what she's doing." Pastor Eddie asked him, "Who's influencing you?"

My husband didn't tell him anything, but I knew. I tried to talk with him, and asked, "Are you doing this because you have been corrected?"

The strife grew; one day he told me he needed to talk to me. My husband told me, "I'm leaving."

I looked at him and said, "Where are you going? Can't you see we have been so blessed; we have a church, a men's and women's home. People are growing and getting stronger in Jesus. Look at this great work!"

"I'm leaving," he repeated, "I'm going to Bosnia; the military called me and wants me to come back in."

I stood there, staring at him. I knew the military hadn't called him; I knew he'd called the military and asked for an assignment. A few days later, he was in his military uniform, along with his suitcases, and said, "I need a ride to the airport in Seattle." We drove to the airport almost in silence. I didn't know what to think. I was tired of arguing and fighting; I couldn't take it anymore.

They say that absence makes the heart grow fonder, but in this case it was different. He didn't go into Bosnia; he went into Germany, and that story is not important- it's over and past. After a couple of months of prayer, I decided to fly into Germany to spend time, talk, and try to work our problems through. Again there was so much tension and continual arguing, all because I was a woman preacher. I couldn't believe he just walked out and left for Germany, and didn't care enough to stick around and fight it through.

A few other things I don't want to mention in this book happened, before I left Germany. I told him, "You have two months to come home and work this marriage through, or I will file for divorce."

He just looked at me, and said, "You won't file for divorce; you're a Christian, and you have a church."

"Yes: first, it's not *my* church, it's *God's* Church! Second, I'm not a *stupid* Christian." I headed back to the airport, and flew back home. I wasn't sure what was going to happen.

I received a call from Dr. Cho's secretary; she told me, "I'm sorry for bothering you. I had a dream last night, and I had to call you." She began to share with me a word from God, "You are going to go through a very dark time- it will seem as if it is so dark- close your eyes, and lift up your hand. God will carry you through."

She didn't know what was going on. I knew this woman was a prayer warrior, even though I didn't understand all she was telling me was just about to happen. But I kept her words in my heart.

Three months went by; my husband did not return. By this time Jill had come to live in Oregon, along with Beverly, who'd been second in charge of the women's homes before in Colorado. She now was placed in charge of the homes in Oregon.

Jill was surprised at everything that was happening; I finally told her the whole story. No one knew about the tension between my husband and me- not *one* person- except the pastor we were counseling with. But I finally opened up and shared with Jill all that was going on, and that I was going to file for divorce.

HELL SCREAMS, "FAILURE!"

13

Psalm 6:6; "I am weary with my groaning; all night I make my bed swim; I drench my couch with my tears."

I finally sat down with a few of the church leaders and shared with them what was going on. I shared how my husband had been disciplined, and asked to step down for a few months, but he'd left instead. I was surprised by their kind and compassionate response. These were men and women who had now been with me for almost two years since the church split. They didn't know the entire battle that had gone on, but they knew that I loved them.

Pastor Eddie came to visit me, and asked if I was okay; he shared with me how he felt God spoke to his heart about my situation. He then asked me a strange question, "Who is the baby's mother?"

I could only look at him, not comprehending what he was asking me. Then he asked again, "Who is the baby's mother?"

I just looked at him again, and said, "I don't know what you mean."

"Who birthed this church?"

"God!" I replied.

"Yes," he replied, "God, but you're the mother of this church." Then he asked, "How much do you love this church and people?"

"I love them with all my heart."

"Do you love them enough to not see them cut in two?"

"YES!"

He shared, "You should close the church down, and place the people in other good churches."

By this time, the church had grown to over 125 people. My heart sank! I gazed at him and pondered... I knew he loved Jesus. Then I thought about the church split, and all we had been through before. I knew I didn't want to see anyone hurt again. I started to tear up. I knew what he was saying; these people would be right in the middle of a divorce.

♪❀

I met with the leaders; they were now home group leaders, with about 8 to 10 people in each group. I explained to them what Pastor Eddie had shared with me. I let them know that I loved them with all my heart, and that we needed to look out for the new converts.

I wrote a letter of recommendation for each leader, directed to their new pastors for whichever church they decided to attend. The letters requested, "Please welcome this home leader, love them and know they are very special, and I know they will be a great blessing to your church."

This parting was *so hard!* I said my good-byes to everyone, sharing how much I loved them, and encouraging them to please be faithful to their home group leaders; they would take care of them.

I then closed the doors of the church, and stopped having service. I had already filed for the divorce, and every morning I still went into the church for prayer. I wept for hours each day. I felt like I had truly failed. Jill, Beverly, and my daughter Kaweah were being strong; I told them to please go find a church. They visited a few churches, but always came back, not saying very much. They knew I was broken and hurting.

ﾉﾟ

Divorce is like someone taking a baseball bat and swinging it as hard as they can, against a giant high-rise building made out of all glass windows. It starts to crack; the noise you hear sounds low at first. Then, abruptly, the noise increases as the glass shatters from that one crack into a million different directions, cracking from the bottom to the top of that high-rise building, until it's broken into uncountable pieces.

It was crazy. Divorce is not easy for anyone; it affects everything and everyone around.

ﾉﾟ

Before I was married I was a widow. I had made investments. I owned my own home before we were married. I never once thought about a prenuptial agreement; who gets a "prenup" as a Christian? When you say, "I do," in marriage, it's supposed to be "until death do us part". After we were married, I was excited about building a work for God in Oregon. I turned over some of those investments I had from before, and bought land in Oregon. This helped buy houses for the women's and men's homes. I'd bought a warehouse, which was rented out to bring in extra money, for helping reach more people and preach the gospel. I'd bought a church property in a prime commercial location, which came with a house and a separate office. Then we'd bought a beautiful old log cabin on six acres to live in.

I hadn't thought about what could happen if someone walked out. I put both our names on everything, thinking nothing about it. Of course, we blended our monies together when we were married. But the purchases of most of these investments were only made possible because before I was married, I had property already, and sold it to invest in Oregon property and the future of the ministry. I never worried about receiving monies from the church; it hadn't mattered to me, one way or another. I loved ministry, and had always loved ministry; I didn't preach or minister for money. Everything I did was for the purpose of expanding the Kingdom of God. Now here I was, right in the middle of a divorce.

This bombshell really hit hard: I found out my pastor from Colorado was now giving my husband counsel by phone, telling him to take me to court. "Take everything you can from her; she shouldn't be preaching, she's a woman..." My husband never told the pastor that he had been corrected and told to step down for a season, with pastoral counseling.

When I found out that my pastor was now telling him to take me to court to fight against me, I felt like a knife went right through my heart. I wanted to die! I couldn't believe it. Now, unexpectedly, lawyers had to get involved. I found myself getting so angry. I didn't like what I was feeling in my heart. I'd been delivered from anger, and I'd been saved now, for 17 years, but I felt this anger trying so hard to come back. I had to fight that demon everyday going through this trial.

Then I found out that my husband was going around to people, telling them he was going to start the church over again. He started fellowshipping and partnering with the couple who'd split the church before. I thought, "My GOD, HELP ME!"

My lawyer told me it could take up to a year to get through the divorce. ONE YEAR!

There was no way I could just sit in this empty church morning after morning, broken and hurting, just waiting to see what was going to happen in court, or wade through all the betrayal again.

I called Pastor Eddie. He told me, "Your pastor from Colorado is pushing your husband against you."

I asked, "What should I do?"

"Maybe you should leave the area, find a new place to start over, and return for court dates."

"I need to pray!"

I hung up the phone, and just cried like a baby. I was hurt, angry, and scared. HOW DID ALL THIS HAPPEN? Where was I going to go? I couldn't go back to Colorado. I didn't have much money on me. What money I had was now being spent on court and my attorney. My daughter, Kaweah, was still in college; all the girls from the women's home were relocated and moved out, except for one; her name was Lisa, a beautiful 6'1" black girl. I had found her many years before, living outside a dumpster trashcan, in the parking lot of McDonald's, in the cold of a Colorado Springs winter.

When I first met Lisa in Colorado, she had been raped and sexually abused by her brothers. Later, she had been forced to sell her body. I brought her into my women's home. When she was there at first, I knew she must have been abused for many years. She wouldn't sleep in the bed for months, but would sleep sitting up in the corner of the bedroom, wrapped in layers of big men's jackets, zipped up to her neck to cover up her perfect shape. I realized that Lisa had the mind of a 6- to

10-year-old. She was now living with me in Oregon. She was
doing so well, faithful to church, and had been with me now for
over 12 years. She was like an extra daughter; I certainly
couldn't leave her behind in Oregon.

I felt so defeated, like a failure. I failed! It was like hell opened
up its gates, and I felt like every demon from hell was coming
up out of the pit, screaming into my ear: "FAILURE, FAILURE!
YOU'RE WORTHLESS! You're a Christian, you failed!" Those
demons were not letting up.

A few people who had come to church before were trying to
make contact with me, but I couldn't let them into the middle
of all this insanity.

I sat down with Kaweah, Jill, and Beverly, and told them that I
needed to leave town. I neither wanted to hurt these people,
nor have them feel like they needed to pick sides. The girls
asked me, "Where are you going?"

I couldn't answer them; I didn't know where I was going. I had
thought we were going to build an awesome ministry, with a
Prayer Mountain in Oregon. Now, everything was shattered.

I told them, "I need to leave the state." I had been praying,
crying out to God, "Please, help me Father!"

I packed a few things, told Beverly, Kaweah, and Jill I was going
to leave to find a new place to live, and that I would return in a
few weeks. Beverly was working, and Kaweah was still
attending college.

Jill said, "Pastor, you can't go by yourself. I'm going with you."
She had her bag packed in a flash, and it was in the car.

I told her, "I don't know where I'm going."

She smiled and said, "Oh well, then we shall go nowhere
together; you can't go by yourself." I felt so beat up inside, I
couldn't argue with her.

The next morning, with a US road map, we started on the road, Jill and I. My plan was to go across the whole United States until I heard a word from the Lord. We headed south towards California; I stopped at every major city. Each location I stopped at, I prayed for a few days asking the Lord, and heard nothing. We stayed in a hotel in each city, and I'd be praying, *"Lord,* where do you want me?" I stopped in San Francisco, Sacramento, Los Angeles, Orange County, before we drove into San Diego, California.

When we landed in the heart of San Diego, I stopped at Hotel Circle, and rented a room for a few days at Motel 6. I was praying and fasting, "Lord, where do you want me?"

On the third day, I felt the Holy Spirit speak something to my heart, "Behold, there is much land". What a strange thought to come into my mind! I had never been to San Diego before. I prayed again for what seemed like hours, and felt the same thing come again to my heart.

Jill knew I needed time to pray every day. I truly needed healing inside, and I needed direction. She would find someplace to go, giving me hours alone in the hotel room to read and pray. I got up off the floor after praying and went to find Jill. I shared with her what I felt in my spirit and heart. She grinned and said, "Praise God! I was worried you might want to drive into Mexico next."

Those words- *"Behold, there is much land"*- that's all that was spoken to my heart. I didn't know what those words meant, but I held them fast. I checked on a two-bedroom apartment before I left San Diego and headed back to Oregon. I talked to the manager, and he promised he would have an apartment available and ready when I returned from Oregon. My drive back to Oregon was long, with a million thoughts going through my head. A court date needed to be set. Divorce! The people! What was going to happen?

When I returned to Oregon, I knew I needed to pack and leave as soon as possible. It was too hard for me to be in Oregon- oh, the pain in my heart! -I felt like everything had crumbled around me.

I sat down with Kaweah, and told her that I was moving to San Diego. I suggested she should finish up her college in Oregon.

She said, "Mom, I love you, but you are *not* leaving me behind; you need me."

"I have nothing to offer you, Kaweah; I don't know what's going to happen."

A smile, a big hug: "We're going to get through this together."

Next I told Beverly I was leaving. She had a great job at the university, but she too said, "You're not leaving me behind. You need me."

Jill had already declared the same to me, earlier.

And, of course, I wasn't leaving Lisa behind; who would watch over her? She was packed, and beaming as if we were going on a vacation. Her young mind really didn't comprehend everything that was happening.

When we arrived in California, I found out the apartment manager had lied to me. He'd rented the apartment that he'd promised to hold till we got there.

So here we were: five women, with a big U-Haul, a car, and no place to live, in California. I couldn't believe this! We were tired. I told the ladies to just pull over and rest, jumped back into the car, and called a few different apartments in the area; there was *nothing*. As I was driving back to the truck, I noticed a small "For Rent" sign, in front of a little studio cottage. I called the number, met with the owner, told him the apartment we'd been promised was rented; if he would please allow us to rent this cottage on the Main Street? - and we would later use it only for our office. He was very nice; the papers were drawn up, and I signed a year lease.

We found a storage place, put all our furniture in storage, emptied the truck out and returned it to the rental, before they could charge us for another day. We took only our sleeping bags, individual suitcases, and a desk so we could set up our computer in the cottage. Now then! -five women, sleeping in a 20 by 30, one room studio cottage- everyone in their sleeping bags on the floor. All kept a good attitude; at least we had our own little kitchen and bathroom. We ended up having to live in this condition for about a week.

In time, we were finally set up in a two-bedroom apartment. One day while I was out getting a few things done, Jill found two sets of bunk beds and placed them in one room. When I got home, she showed me, "This is our room."

All four women were in one room. I told Jill, "You can't do that, it's too crowded!"

"We all decided you need time to pray, read, and get the mind of God." Jill told me, "We are all going to get jobs, and you are going to pray and read every day until we get through all this divorce stuff."

Fighting back tears, and swallowing the lump in my throat, I told them, "Thank you." That night, and every night, for one year I cried myself to sleep. I would wake up early every morning and pray. I'd pray all morning long until noon, break for lunch, and then start praying again, until almost 5 p.m. I was so broken inside; all I could do was pray in the spirit. I was shattered inside, and needed a miracle in my heart.

Every day I fought the demons from hell who whispered into my head, screaming at me over and over, "YOU ARE A FAILURE. YOU ARE WORTHLESS!"

My court dates in Oregon were still months away...

I had nearly forgotten one thing; over a year before all this divorce stuff happened, I had organized a Crusade, which was to be held at the downtown Phoenix Convention Center. The arrangements had already been paid for, and five churches had committed to attend the three-day meeting. I'd thought about cancelling it, but it was too late. I decided, "I'm going to do this."

When we arrived, the 3,000 chairs had been set up; the platform and everything was in place. I flew in some amazing old friends to help me with the worship: Steve Arnold, one of the best worship leaders and a great vocalist; Bart Edmonds, an excellent bass player; and Al Boyce, an amazing drummer. Our team of Jill, Beverly, and Kaweah knew what to do. Everything was set up for the first night.

I hadn't shared with anyone in Arizona that I was right in the middle of a divorce; I felt too much shame. I'd booked this meeting, long before it all had started, and I couldn't just not show up. The first night I entered the Convention Center, I walked to a little back waiting room behind the platform.

I could hear the worship starting, Kaweah was singing with Steve, and they sounded wonderful! I was as nervous as ever. There was a small knock on the door. It was Jill; as she walked in, I could tell something was different on her face.

She asked me in her sweet, gentle voice, "Why do you preach?"

I answered her, "To see lives saved and touched by Jesus."

Smiling, she asked again, "Why do you preach?"

Looking at her, I swallowed the lump in my throat. She reached over and placed a hand on my shoulder, and then looked at me right in the eye, saying, "When you go out there, you remember why you are preaching. Look only at the front row. I know God's going to use you tonight- powerfully."

I knew something was wrong, and just looked at her: "No one came, did they?"

With a tear in her eye, she said, "YES! There are people sitting out on that front row who need Jesus. *You* remember *why* you are preaching!"

What I hadn't known was that the churches had called and said they would not attend or support the meetings, because I had "left" my husband. Jill and Beverly had received the calls and didn't want to break my heart by telling me this the night I was to preach. They went out into the rough area, and searched for as many people as they could find- town drunks, as many prostitutes as they came across- who were gathered up for the meeting.

The worship was tremendous; when it ended, before I stepped out onto the platform, Jill spoke to me, "We are excited to see all that the Holy Spirit is going to do tonight!"

I swallowed that GREAT BIG LUMP in my throat, and walked out onto the platform. I looked only once out at all those empty chairs, then I remembered Jill's voice, "On the front row are people who need Jesus; remember why you're preaching." I kept my eyes only on the front row that night. Yes, about 25 people were saved every night- they were saved, healed and filled with the Holy Spirit. The first night after preaching, I went back to my hotel. I sat in a chair and placed my head in my lap, and cried like a baby.

That devil still screamed in my ear, "Failure! Failure! Failure!"

Jill walked in, and sat across from me. She smiled, and gently said, "25 people were saved tonight. That's why we came, right?" She continued, "I'm sorry. I didn't have the heart to tell you, that at the last minute the churches received a call from the pastor in Colorado. He told them, *'Don't support* her; she left her husband.' They said they couldn't support the meeting."

I started to weep. About 90 people showed up all together, those three nights. When I look back today, I can now smile. Why? Because, how many preachers do you know who preached to 2,910 empty seats?

That was not the only rumor that was spread; words came back to my ears always- evil, wicked, lies.

❧❧❧❧❧❧❧❧❧❧❧❧❧❧❧❧❧❧❧❧❧❧❧❧❧❧❧❧

The day before the last court for the settlement of the divorce, the Holy Spirit spoke to my heart, "If any man asks for your jacket, give it to them."

At first I wanted to *scream,* "NO, JESUS! NO! It's not fair!"

Because I had labored for Jesus, not caring if I received a recorded monthly paycheck in my name, it looked like I hadn't put any monies into all the property that I'd purchased. Since the judge was former military, he was favoring my husband. When he walked into the court with his full dress uniform, and the judge addressed him as, "Sir," I knew right then I was in trouble.

That day I decided to let everything I owned go in my heart, no matter what would happen. Was everything completely and fairly divided? No! But in a divorce is anything fairly divided? Divorce is ugly. But it was final. I had to get through this, and I knew I had to start all over. What did I do to deserve all this? What was I guilty of?

I was *A Woman Called of God* to preach the gospel of Jesus Christ to the lost and broken-hearted.

"Get Up, I Said, Get Up!"

14

Psalm 30:1-5; "I will extol You, O Lord, for You have lifted me up, and have not let my foes rejoice over me. O Lord my God, I cried out to You, and You have healed me. O Lord, You have brought my soul up from the grave; You have kept me alive, that I should not go down to the pit. Sing praise to the Lord, you saints of His, and give thanks at the remembrance of His holy name. For His anger is but for a moment, His favor is for life; weeping may endure for a night, but joy comes in the morning."

The divorce was final. I was given the rights to the church building, but it was too late. The building was now empty, and all it held were memories:

Memories, of…

Smiles, laughter, and tears of joy from those who had answered an altar call…

Surrendered hearts to a God who is always faithful, a God who is faithful to hear a cry in desperate need of a miracle…

Morning prayers that echoed through those walls, I'm sure right into heaven, to Jesus our Advocate…

Songs of praise, which were sung in that building with our whole hearts- I know they touched God's ears...

Hundreds of lives, touched by the Holy Spirit in that building, won't go unnoticed in heaven...

Selling this building was hard, but it was a must.

❧ ❧

I placed it on the market, and it was not long before a buyer came to purchase it. I sold the building and paid every overdue debt, paid off the balance of all loans owed on the building. Then I gave away all the money which was left over to other ministries. I thought it was over, because I had failed.

The drive back to California was hard; I felt like I had been in a boxing ring, beaten up round after round, and then in the final round, taken the knockout punch. The Devil counted 1-2-3-4-5-6-7-8-9-10, and I was down; I couldn't get up.

Jill was with me on the final court day, and we didn't say much on that long drive back to California. She knew I was so broken inside. I couldn't tell anyone what really had happened- I wanted *no one* in the middle- but now it was all over.

When we finally arrived at the apartment in California, I thought to myself, "Five women!" Then they asked me, "How did everything go?" By my expression they knew.

My attorney was right; it took a little over a year to get through all this mess. When I drove that final drive out of Oregon, I left with a broken heart, broken promises, a U-Haul, a credit card, and empty pockets. What happened to the vision?! What was I going to *do?* No one invited me to preach, because the pastor in Colorado had told many others about my divorce.

Sunday was right around the corner.

"Please go find a church to lock into, get involved," I told the girls, finally, "You need to listen to me. I failed, and now as a Christian I'm divorced. No one wants me as a preacher or as an evangelist; you saw the meeting back in Arizona. People are telling others I left with all the money."

I'd heard one lie after another, like a razor to my heart. The lies kept piling up; old friends were rude, calling me up to ridicule. They didn't ask me what really happened; they didn't want the truth. And I was at a point where I was so sick of it all, I didn't care to wade through the lies they had been told. Some were even calling me and asking, "Why did you leave town with another man?"

So many lies, one after another, kept coming back to me. I felt so defeated inside.

I told the girls, "I'm sorry! Please go find a church!"

Jill would tell me, "You need time to pray; God's faithful- *please go pray.*"

It was now over a year and a half, and I was still weeping almost every night. My pillow was truly filled with tears. What did I do? All I wanted to do was preach the gospel of Jesus Christ, and win the lost to Jesus. I still heard those demons from hell, *screaming* in my ear, "You're nothing but a FAILURE!"

I stepped down from ministry. I was still praying every day, weeping for what seemed like hours every day in the Spirit. I loved Jesus with all my heart. I found myself telling God every day, "I'm so sorry for the church not working out, please forgive me." Telling Him, "I'm sorry for my marriage not working." I was filled with guilt, shame, and defeat. I thought to myself, "In time, I will find a good church; I will lock in and help build the kingdom of God."

One day there was a knock on the door; it was Pastor Eddie. I'd neither seen nor talked with Pastor Eddie and his wife for a few months since the divorce was final. He looked at me and asked, *"What are you doing?"*

"Nothing," I replied, "I stepped down from ministry. I failed as a Christian, plus now I'm divorced. No one wants me to preach for them; all my meetings have been canceled."

He gazed at me, as I started to tear up. "LOOK AT ME!" he exclaimed, "LOOK AT ME! GET UP! You need to get up, you didn't fail, YOU NEED TO GET UP! Or you will stand before God with a greater judgment. You have a call on your life, and you'd better fulfill that call or you will stand before God and give account for *not* doing what He has called you to!

I had tears running down my face, as I looked up at him and asked, "How? I tried! I'm a woman."

ℐﻬ

What happened afterwards was a miracle of God's love, faithfulness, and grace. Pastor Eddie called someone from the International Church of the Foursquare Gospel denomination. I was later enrolled into Life Bible College. I studied hard every day. On the day of graduation, I stood with many others, both men *and* women called to preach the gospel of Jesus Christ. As they called my name and I walked forward, I was surrounded by amazing, silver-haired, mighty men of God, heroes of the faith. They smiled at me, handed me my ministry diploma, and then told me, "God has called you, and we're behind you, woman of God, 'Go *forth* and preach the gospel to every living creature.'"

I began weeping as these powerful strong men of God surrounded me and anointed me with oil, prayed over me, and commissioned me to preach the Gospel of Jesus Christ. I stood weeping like a baby, tears of joy rolling down my face like a river.

A few years later, I also attended classes at Oral Roberts University, and the same thing happened. Powerful, strong, men of God called out my name; as I walked forward, they handed me my ministerial diploma, laid hands, and anointed me with oil. These mighty men of God spoke God's Word over each one of our lives, and sent us out to different parts of the world to fulfill God's call on our lives, to preach the gospel of Jesus Christ.

It wasn't long after, that I found out my pastor in Colorado had been under the International Church of the Foursquare Gospel denomination for many years. He had pulled out about the second year after I was saved. He knew the truth all along; God has always called both men and women into His service.

He had been under the Foursquare denomination, which was founded by a woman named Aimee Semple McPherson, a powerful woman of God! Today, her legacy lives on through the thousands of men and women called of God, ordained to preach the gospel of Jesus Christ, sent throughout the whole world to reach a lost and broken world in need of *Jesus*.

THE INVISIBLE BURQA

15

Genesis 1:27-28; "So God created man in His own image; in the image of God He created him; male and female He created them. Then God blessed them, and God said to them, 'Be fruitful and multiply; fill the earth and subdue it; have dominion over the fish of the sea, over the birds of the air, and over every living thing that moves on the earth."

As I write this book, I have been saved for 35 years. I have learned some very valuable lessons- lessons that will stay with me for a lifetime. Prayer has been one of the greatest lessons, for without prayer I wouldn't be writing this book today. I thank God for the Holy Spirit, His love, His wisdom, and His comfort.

Prayer is what keeps us secure in times of trouble.

*"When you are hardest hit,
you must never quit!"*

*Quitting is not an option. You may be crawling, and feel you're breathing your last breath, and may even feel you're almost dead. Don't stop praying, trusting, and believing. Don't go into sin; always-----**pray.** God is always listening, and He collects our tears. In your darkest trials, and when tests come into your*

Christian walk, keep walking! Don't give one inch of your life to the devil, by giving up on God's promises.

My whole purpose in writing this book is to share about women called of God. Up to this point, I've had to bring my story to light, in order to share this message from my heart, in these last few chapters.

ᏕᎠ

Can women preach? Can they pastor a church? Did Jesus tell women to shut up and get married? What was Paul saying to Timothy about women? Are women to be silent in the church?

Three verses in the Bible keep women in captivity, in a position where many are told to be silent, shut up, or keep a cover over their head. The Lord gave me the idea for the cover of this book. At first I thought, "Holy Spirit, what are you saying?"

The burqa is something I don't really understand. The more the Holy Spirit began to speak to me, the more I pondered, "Why the cover?"

With the population of the world today peaking upwards to 7 billion people, the Holy Spirit spoke to my heart, "Half of my people are kept from fulfilling My purpose."

Luke 19:9-10: "And Jesus said to him, 'today salvation has come to this house, because he also is a son of Abraham; for the Son of Man has come to seek and to save that which was lost.'"

Satan has used assumptions, long-standing traditions, private opinions, wrongful and faulty interpretations, and allowed additions to be called the Word of God. Satan has had a good time with this lie to hold women back, those whom God Himself has called for His service.

ᏕᎠ

Matthew 28:18-20: *"And Jesus came and spoke to* **them**, *saying,* *"All authority has been given to Me in heaven and on earth. Go therefore and make disciples of all the nations, baptizing* **them** *in the name of the Father and of the Son and of the Holy Spirit, teaching* **them** *to observe all things that I have commanded you; and lo, I am with you always, even to the end of the age." Amen.*

Luke 24:45-49: *"And He opened their understanding, that they might comprehend the Scriptures. Then He said to them, "Thus it is written, and thus it was necessary for the Christ to suffer and to rise from the dead the third day, and that repentance and remission of sins should be preached in His name to all nations, beginning at Jerusalem. And you are witnesses of these things. Behold, I send the promise of My Father upon you; but tarry in the city of Jerusalem until you are endued with power from on high."*

That wonderful experience was fulfilled in the upper room, as recorded here:

Acts 1:13-17: *"And when they had entered, they went up into the upper room where they were staying: Peter, James, John, and Andrew; Philip and Thomas; Bartholomew and Matthew; James the son of Alphaeus and Simon the Zealot; and Judas the son of James. These all continued with one accord in prayer and supplication,* **with the women and Mary the mother of Jesus,** *and with His brothers. And in those days Peter stood up in the midst of the disciples (altogether the number of names was about a hundred and twenty), and said, "Men and brethren, this Scripture had to be fulfilled, which the Holy Spirit spoke before by the mouth of David concerning Judas, who became a guide to those who arrested Jesus..."*

Acts 2:1-4:"When the Day of Pentecost had fully come, **they were** **all** *with one accord in one place. And suddenly there came a sound from heaven, as of a rushing mighty wind, and it filled the whole house where they were sitting. Then there appeared to them divided tongues, as of fire, and one sat upon* **each of**

***them**. And **they were all filled** with the Holy Spirit and began to speak with other tongues, as the Spirit gave them utterance."*

ﾠﾠﾠﾠﾠﾠﾠﾠﾠﾠﾠﾠﾠﾠﾠﾠﾠﾠﾠﾠﾠﾠﾠﾠﾠﾠﾠﾠ

Satan's goal is to stop you, man or woman, from fulfilling your God-given call. When I look back at all I went through, I realize the plan of the devil was to get me to throw in the towel, and give up the fight.

Genesis 50:20: "But as for you, you meant evil against me; but God meant it for good, in order to bring it about as it is this day, to save many people alive."

When Joseph went through all that he'd been through, God had a bigger plan. Yes, it was painful for Joseph. Yes, it was *very* painful for me. Today, I thank God for **all** those people who helped shape me to become who God wanted me to be.

How could I help others who have been rejected? My life was set apart for God's purpose from the day I was saved. If it had not been for the grace of God's never ending love, and all those who rejected me, I wouldn't be where I am today.

Have I forgiven them? - Those who tried to stop me, and nearly succeeded, causing me to question my calling? Yes indeed! I forgave all those who lied and hurt me years ago.

Unforgiveness would have been my own tombstone.

Forgiveness is a stepping-stone up, a step above all the devil's plans of destruction. The devil's plan has always been to stop God's plan for mankind. Satan is jealous when someone comes to Jesus Christ, and even more jealous of our calling. We become his target, but hold on, because there is *victory!*

Satan, from the beginning of time, has wanted everything God has and stands for. He coveted God's authority in heaven. If we don't understand our enemy and how the devil works, then we can become a victim of his evil plots.

Let's first look at some of Satan's evil working:

Isaiah 14:12-14: "How you are fallen from heaven, O Lucifer, son of the morning! How you are cut down to the ground, you who weakened the nation! For you have said in your heart: 'I will ascend into heaven, I will exalt my throne above the stars of God; I will also sit on the mount of the congregation on the farthest sides of the north; I will ascend above the heights of the clouds, I will be like the Most High.'"

Satan always tries to stop God's plan, right from the start. He didn't waste any time. In the garden he goes to work very quickly, to taint and destroy God's plan for mankind. *Why?* Because when God created mankind, both men and women, He gave *them both*, God's authority.

We can see the serpent, Satan, getting Eve to question the goodness of God. (*Genesis 3:1, "Has GOD indeed said...,")*

Eve, with Adam her husband, ate from the very tree God had told them not to eat. **They** disobeyed God's command, by eating from the tree they were told NOT to eat from. Did *that* tree look any different from the other trees in the garden? Was it a different color? I believe it looked just like any other tree in the garden,

> *but that one tree represented God's authority.*

God gave man a free will; He gave them the very best of all He made. But Satan was jealous of mankind. He was jealous of the *authority* that had been given to both the man and woman, Adam and Eve, by God Himself.

*Genesis 1:27-28: "So God created man in His own image; in the image of God He created him; male and female He created them. Then God **blessed them**, and God said to them, "Be fruitful and multiply; fill the earth and subdue it; **have dominion** over the fish of the sea, over the birds of the air, and over every living thing that moves on the earth."*

God gave them both: **man/woman equal authority over the earth,** and all He created. This was God's original plan for mankind. One man with one woman, loving one another, having children, multiplying more children, and they were called to rule. One did not rule over the other; they walked side-by-side in the beautiful garden God created for them. It was God's perfect plan.

When God said, "Let us make man," was He referring to just the man Adam, or to all humanity? This is very important because God said, "man," would rule His creation. If the first physical man, Adam, is meant, it stands to reason that *Eve,* made later, would then be part of the creation he would rule. *But* let's remember! God's command was given *to them*, not him. God's original statement must govern our thinking on this subject! *Ha' Adam*, with the definite article *ha*, used in:

*Genesis 1:26,27: "Then God said, 'Let Us make **man** in Our image, according to Our likeness; let **them** have dominion over the fish of the sea, over the birds of the air, and over the cattle, over all the earth and over every creeping thing that creeps on the earth.' So God created **man** in His own image; in the image of God He created him; **male and female** He created **them**."*

Ha'adam, is a generic term meaning "humanity" or "mankind." That's why the plural term "them" is used. If God meant a single person, the pronoun "I," "he," or "him" would have been used, but not "them." This tells us that God did not give His command to rule just to one person, but to all humanity, including the *soon* to be made woman. Satan has twisted the word of God for years to *stop* God's plan of spreading the gospel message into the entire world. Do you really think Satan is going to *stop* now? Of course not! He has but a short time left. And it's time the other half of God's kingdom, the women, to be released to preach the word of God to a lost and dying world in need of *Jesus.*

Why did it take me so long to have this understanding? *Satan* is very crafty. Why are so many Christian churches in America caught up in this evil lie, and keeping women in an invisible burqa?

Many have used the lie, "it was just Eve who disobeyed God." Yet, Satan caused *both* Adam and Eve to yield to the temptation; *they both* fell. *They both* brought sin into the world (a *curse).* *They both* disobeyed God, and through their disobedience we see what was about to take place **_because of the curse of sin._**

In Genesis Chapter Three, the consequences of Adam and Eve's disobedience were immediate. Please read these verses a few times until you understand how *very* important they are concerning women. Remember what is happening; God is telling all three- the serpent, Eve, and Adam- what would happen next. There would be consequences for their disobedience; the curse came because of their willingness to disobey His command, "Don't eat of the tree of the knowledge of good and evil."

We can see the horrendous devastation and the consequences of the curse. At the same exact time, God knew the devil's tricks, and in His great love for you and me, He'd made a plan to redeem mankind from this evil curse. Let's read with understanding:

*Genesis 3:14-19: "So the Lord God said to the serpent: 'Because you have done this (**tempted Eve and Adam**), you are cursed more than all cattle, and more than every beast of the field; on your belly you shall go, and you shall eat dust all the days of your life. And I will put enmity (a deep seated hatred and hostility),* *between you (Satan) and the woman (Mary, the mother of Jesus), and between your seed (seed of* sin, the curse)*and her* **Seed***; (The* birth *of Christ* Jesus)He *(Jesus) shall bruise your head (authority given to you by Adam and Eve), and you shall bruise His heel."*

What authority? Okay- when Eve and Adam willingly disobeyed God by eating from the tree God commanded them to not eat from, there was a death, a *spiritual death.* They gave the authority and dominion of the earth over to Satan through their act of sin. Like a man who is given the title deed of a house, that man becomes the full owner of the house.

The earth God created for mankind was given to Adam and Eve, like the title deed; Adam and Eve were also given God's *authority.* Satan is very tricky; Adam and Eve didn't realize the price of their sin. It would cost them the earth (their title deed- the earth belonged to them). God just created it and gave it to them. Adam and Eve handed over their beautiful, perfect earth, and all that God had created for them; they gave it all to *Satan.*

The earth was now the devil's property. A *curse* of sin and death came to the earth ("in the day you eat, you shall die"). Satan now had rule over mankind; a spiritual *death* came to *all* mankind. Through one man sin came into the world. Adam and Eve had no idea what was about to happen. Like so many today who willingly sin, they never counted the price of the result of their sin.

Genesis 3:16: "To the woman He said: 'I will greatly multiply your sorrow and your conception; in pain you shall bring forth children;'"

God wasn't talking about labor pains during delivery. He was saying that because of her willingness to sin, she brought the curse of sin upon her own child; she would birth the first murderer. Her firstborn son, Cain, would kill his own brother, Abel. Sin was taking its course.

"Your desire shall be for your husband;"

God is continuing to address the result of their *sin,* the curse, which entered the world. Eve's love would no longer be satisfied by God's love, but now her flesh would be in want. Why do we find so many women today feeling empty unless they have a man in their life? Why do so many women run from man to man, looking for love? Because of the curse... their love would no longer be satisfied and focused on the Lord, but instead the desire for a man.

Having over 500 women come through our women's homes through the years helped me to see this vicious cycle. Until a woman knows her worth comes only in Christ, she will never be complete. I have also seen many married women; when their relationship with God is not strong, they can drive their husbands crazy. I've counseled many couples, broken and hurting; the husband is usually the one trying so hard to jump through hoops to make his wife happy. I explain to the wife, "Your husband is great, he's fantastic, he's Superman, he's unbelievable, but he is not God." Married women live under the curse without realizing it. A married woman must build her relationship with Jesus first in order to have a *great* relationship with her husband.

I have felt sorry for so many married men, whose wives have become like a leech (ladies, please don't get mad at me; there *is* freedom!). Without realizing Satan's tricks, they get stuck, sucking the very life out of their husbands, and they hinder what could be a beautiful relationship in marriage.

All women, when they come to Jesus, must rebuke the curse and build a strong relationship with Christ. When a woman understands she must be complete in Christ first, only then will she be ready for marriage, or if married, can she allow her husband to be free to love her the way Jesus intended in His original plan.

"And he shall rule over you:"

Many years ago when I owned a store, I watched a couple as they were shopping; up and down the aisles they walked. After a little while the woman brought a little item worth about a dollar. She put it on the counter at the same time her husband walked up. She turned around and smiled at him, then he asked, "What's that?" Then in front of everyone he lifted his voice, "You don't need that, put it away!" The woman turned beet red, and said in her soft voice, "It's only one dollar." He yelled at her like she was his kid, and said, "Put that away now." Then he put a few things on the counter and she stood there, like a puppy that had been whipped, with its tail between its legs. They walked out the door. I reached over for the item, put it in a bag, walked out to the car, and said, "Excuse me." She turned and I handed her the item she'd wanted. Smiling from ear to ear she said, "Thank you," and got into the car. I wanted to say something to him, but I knew it would only make it worse for her when she got home.

Another time, a family was right in the middle of a little, normal squabble. The adult kids were fighting back and forth; the father stood up and began to stand up for one of the sons. At one point the mother stood up and said, "Maybe we should look at the whole picture, dear." All of a sudden I saw the father, her husband, point his finger at his wife. She had birthed him seven children, who were now grown adults. He pointed up towards the stairs and yelled at his wife, "Get to your room!" She tried to talk again, but he yelled in a stern voice, "I said, go to your room NOW!" I just stood there, and I too dismissed myself (I might have found myself in another room next to his wife).

These examples show a terrible pattern: this "I wear the pants in this house" attitude was very ugly. In reality, these men mistreated their wives before God and everyone else.

Marriages run into major trouble when they live under this curse, "He shall rule over you." Abuse has become rampant in many marriages, for both Christians and non-Christians. Satan has used for evil the twisted understanding of this one line throughout the ages; it is demonic. I will explain later in more detail about this subject.

Why would any man want to rule over any woman, or any other man for that matter? What causes this problem, this overwhelming driving force to control and rule over another? It's the *curse* that came from Satan, starting in the garden.

This is why we see so much violence in our nation today; this is a major problem. Gangs are rampant in the United States; there are several groups, which include national street gangs, local street gangs, prison gangs, motorcycle gangs, ethnic and organized crime gangs. Approximately 1.4 million people were part of gangs as of 2011, and more than 33,000 gangs were active in the United States.

This demon force of wanting to "rule over" another person, if not recognized, is very evil- no matter whether you're a man or woman. While pastoring, many years ago, there was a woman in our congregation who was bound by this demon force. Her husband was a wonderful man of God. He always was at church, and loved Jesus. One day I saw bruises on him; at first I said nothing. But another day, I noticed that he was very troubled. I pulled him aside and asked him, "Are you okay?"

For sure, he was distressed about something. I told him, "Listen, there is nothing you can say that will make me think evil of you."

He lowered his head and said, "This is an embarrassing problem I have."

I thought maybe he was bound by some sexual sin and felt shamed by it. But to my surprise, he shared how his wife was a husband beater. She had a wicked spirit to rule over her husband, which would wait until he was sleeping. Without notice, she would begin to hit him with sticks, throwing bottles, and even a belt. She had no control over this, and she needed freedom from this demon force.

Now you may laugh, and think, "A *woman* beating a *man*?" Yes.

This happens all the time. It's not reported as much as the women who are abused by their husbands. I have seen, over and over, women treating their husbands with abuse and manipulation. This, too, is from evil.

This is the sin nature of Satan, the curse; pride is behind this evil.

❧❧❧❧❧❧❧❧❧❧❧❧❧❧❧❧❧❧❧❧❧❧❧❧❧❧

So many Christians have a misunderstanding, and are easily swept into wanting to rule over one another. This is very sad to watch. Satan is so tricky; he also has many couples living a lie, even at church:

At home a couple may work together as a team, raising the children, keeping the house together, etc., but at church, the man may feel like his masculinity is threatened if he doesn't "keep his wife in line." *He* must be in charge!

Other times the couple just pretends; the man "rules over" the wife on Sunday morning; once they leave the parking lot however, the car becomes a battleground. She gets mad; she's learned to manipulate or lash out at her husband till she gets her way.

Any of these circumstances promote an out of balance relationship; it goes cross-grain with our spirit man. You know something's not right; you feel the wrong, but you can't put your finger on it.

✧✦✧✦✧✦✧✦✧✦✧✦✧✦✧✦✧✦✧✦✧✦✧✦✧✦✧✦✧✦✧✦✧✦✧✦✧

God made them, man/woman, to walk together to rule *over the earth;* **not** over one another. Many Christians are still living under the curse, even though *Jesus* came and broke the curse for us; this is the *changeless promise of our wonderful Savior Jesus Christ.*

✧✦✧✦✧✦✧✦✧✦✧✦✧✦✧✦✧✦✧✦✧✦✧✦✧✦✧✦✧✦✧✦✧✦✧✦✧

Galatians 3:13-18: "Christ has redeemed us from the curse of the law, having become a curse for us (for it is written, 'Cursed is everyone who hangs on a tree'), that the blessing of Abraham might come upon the Gentiles in Christ Jesus, that we might receive the promise of the Spirit through faith.

*"Brethren, I speak in the manner of men: Though it is only a man's covenant, yet if it is confirmed, no one annuls or adds to it. Now to Abraham and his Seed were the promises made. He does not say, "And to seeds," as of many, but as of one, '**And to your Seed, who is Christ**'. And this I say, that the law, which was four hundred and thirty years later, cannot annul the covenant that was confirmed before by God in Christ, that it should make the promise of no effect. For if the inheritance is of the law, it is no longer of promise; but God gave it to Abraham by promise."*

Jesus redeemed mankind from the curse of sin and death. His love towards us is amazing. He restored mankind (you and me, and all those who have come to Jesus by faith, and have repented of their sins) back to His original plan *from the beginning*:

*Genesis 1:26-28: "Then God said, 'Let Us make man in Our image, according to Our likeness; **let them have dominion** over* *the fish of the sea, over the birds of the air, and over the cattle, over all the earth and over every creeping thing that creeps on the earth.' So God created man in His own image; in the image of God He created him; __male and female He created them__. The God __blessed them__, and God said to them, 'Be fruitful and multiply; fill the earth and subdue it; __have dominion__ over the fish of the sea, over the birds of the air, and over every living thing that moves on the earth.'"*

We are to walk in faith, walk in God's authority, and rule over the earth.

When God speaks to Adam in *Genesis 3:17,* again He is telling Adam that these were the *consequences* of his disobedience:

Genesis 3:17: "Then to Adam He said, 'Because you have heeded the voice of your wife, and have eaten from the tree of which I commanded you, saying, "You shall not eat of it": Cursed is the ground for your sake; in toil you shall eat of it all the days of your life. Both thorns and thistles it shall bring forth for you, and you shall eat the herb of the field. In the sweat of your face you shall eat bread till you return to the ground, for out of it you were taken; for dust you are, and to dust you shall return.'"

The price of their disobedience was far more than what Adam and Eve ever expected.

Because many people lack understanding of these first three chapters in the Bible, there is great confusion and division over women in ministry today. We are not under the curse or the law.

I would love to answer every question in this book about women called to ministry. In the few remaining chapters of this book we will focus on a few significant areas, with more detail, as we start to break everything down!

GIVER OF LIFE

16

I Corinthians 11:16-18: "But if anyone seems to be contentious, we have no such custom, nor do the churches of God. Now in giving these instructions I do not praise you, since you come together not for the better but for the worse. For first of all, when you come together as a church, I hear that there are divisions among you, and in part I believe it."

These next few verses are very important to understand; like a dictionary, one word could have several meanings. We must go back and study how some of these words were used in the time of Apostle Paul when he wrote the letter to the Corinthian church.

Please understand this! I'm not taking away God's authority, because His authority is what will bring the judgment on sinful man. I'm not taking away the authority of a mother and father over their children.

In the corporate world, you have a boss, overseer or project manager. Their value lies in their position to accomplish a task. What I want to help you understand: is there a hierarchy in a Christian marriage?

Definition of hierarchy: any system or persons or things ranked one above another.

Let's look at some of the scriptures Paul wrote:

Galatians 3:28: "There is neither Jew nor Greek, there is neither slave nor free, there is neither male nor female; for you are all one in Christ Jesus."

Ephesians 5:21: "...submitting to one another in the fear of God."

1 Peter 5:5: "Likewise you younger people, submit yourselves to your elders. Yes, all of you be submissive to one another, and be clothed with humility, for 'God resists the proud, but gives grace to the humble."

When Paul uses the word "head", I'm going to explain this very word to you:

Let's go back in time when Jesus began His ministry upon the earth. During his time, the "oral law" of the Jews, called the Talmud, had evolved from Old Testament times to be common practice and readily accepted as the Jewish law. However, the "oral law" with its over 600 added laws, were the regulations handed down orally from one generation to another; they formed the oral law of the Jews.

Jesus refuted their strongly held traditions:

Mark 7:8-9: "'For laying aside the commandment of God, you hold the tradition of men- the washing of pitchers and cups, and many other such things you do.' And He said to them, 'All too well you reject the commandment of God, that you may keep your tradition.'"

Christ makes this very strong distinction: The traditions, the oral law, and therefore, the Talmud **are not** the commandments of God. This is very important in defining the role of women in God's kingdom, especially in New Testament doctrine and ministry position. The traditions of the Talmud explain exactly why women were minimized and barred from ministry in the religion that was created by the scribes and Pharisees, the leaders of the Jewish faith.

Surprisingly, over 2,000 years later, the majority of New Testament churches, especially in the United States, still hold to the Jewish traditions of the Talmud, strongly believing that they are following the commandment of God by silencing women in the church. In church history, women's position in ministry has risen and fallen, like a roller coaster.

The few scriptures that are most often quoted to exclude women from the offices of apostle, prophet, evangelist, pastor, and teacher must all be examined in context, history, and grammar. Bible scholars throughout history study the Bible to prevent a distortion and twisting of God's word. Pursuing false doctrine is very harmful; it places invisible chains and laws on the men and women whom He has called to be laborers in the harvest field. Because of man's traditions and prejudice, many are held back. It is as if there are invisible burqas placed on the heads of God's daughters.

✶✶✶✶✶✶✶✶✶✶✶✶✶✶✶✶✶✶✶✶✶✶✶✶✶✶✶✶✶✶✶✶

First...

We must understand that the Apostle Paul knew both Hebrew and Greek. Paul was a Pharisee who knew Hebrew well; he grew up in Tarsus, a Greek-speaking city. Greek was the Apostle Paul's native tongue. What did Paul mean when he wrote,

I Corinthians 11:3: "But I want you to know that the head of every man is Christ, the head of woman is man, and the head of Christ is God."

Ephesians 5:23: "For the husband is the head of the wife, as also Christ is the head of the church; and He is the Savior of the body."

Throughout the ages, we see where these verses have almost been etched in stone the biblical role for men in the church, society, and the home. Let's take a look at the Greek word, "kephale," (*kef-al-ay'*) translated "head" in the New Testament.

When we think about that word, "head", we think right away- the boss, chief, someone in charge- right? Some modern Greek lexicons, commentaries, and translations use this definition. It carries the understanding of someone in authority.

Maybe we should take a moment to go back and see what Paul meant when he used this word *for these passages* in the Greek, and what it meant to him and his readers. Did "head" in the ancient Greek mean "superior to" or "one having authority"?

> *Lexicographers Liddell, Scott, Jones, and McKenzie give no evidence of such a meaning.*[1]

So if the word "head" does not normally mean "superior to" or "authority over", what does it mean **in those seven** New *Testament passages where Paul uses it as a figure of speech?*

Now there are differences in the lexicons. The most complete Greek lexicon covering Homeric, classic and *koine* Greek is the work by Liddell, Scott, Jones, and McKenzie. Their time was spent on thousands of Greek writings from the period of Homer, about 1000 B.C., to about A.D. 600. This would include New Testament times.

Allow me to also share that another commonly used lexicon is the koine Greek lexicon by Arndt and Gingrich, usually called "Bauer's". It does list "superior rank" as a **_possible_** meaning for "*kephale*".[2]

(There is SO much more I want to share on this very subject, but for time's sake I must try to condense.)

Those who support Bauer's view that "*kephale*" meant "superior rank" point to the Greek translation of the Old

Testament as evidence that this meaning of *"kephale"* was familiar to Greek-speaking people in New Testament times.

But, the facts do not support that argument; 180 times in the Old Testament the word, *"ro'sh"* (head) is used with the idea of superior rank, chief, leader. They used it the way English-speaking people use "head".

Stay with me; I'm trying to make this as simple as possible to help you understand. Those who translated the Hebrew Old Testament into Greek between 250 and 150 B.C., *rarely used "kephale" for "head".* When they needed to use the word that meant "head" they usually used the Greek word *"archon"*, *which meant* "leader, ruler, and commander". In only 17 places out of 180 did they use *"kephale"*.

"Kephale" is not used much when *ro'sh* carries the idea of authority. Greek translators realized that *"kephale"* did *not* carry the same "leader" or "superior rank" meaning for "head".

HOLD ON, you're about to dance! Okay, what was Paul saying in these *two verses?*

I Corinthians 11:3: *"But I want you to know that the head(source or beginning or completion; giver of life) of every man is Christ, the head(source or beginning or completion; giver of life) of woman is man, and the head(source or beginning or completion; giver of life) of Christ is God."*

Ephesians 5:23: *"For the husband is the head(source or beginning or completion; giver of life) of the wife, as also Christ is the head(source or beginning or completion; giver of life)of the church; and He is the Savior of the body."*

Kephale means:*"Source or beginning or completion; giver of life"*. Paul is using *kephale* with common Greek meanings.

Every place where Paul used *"kephale"* he was writing to Greek-speaking people in cities where most Christians were converts from Greek religions. Since Paul spoke Greek, he would likely write to Greek-speaking Christians, using *Greek* words with Greek meanings they would easily understand.

What Paul meant in those scriptures was not, "head" or "superior rank"; instead it was "**source or beginning or completion; giver of life**". Let's look at a few other verses:

*Colossians 1:18: "And He is the **head** "kephale" of the body, the church, **who is the beginning**, the firstborn from the dead, that in all things He may have the preeminence."*

*Colossians 2:19: "And not holding fast to the **Head**, from whom all the body, nourished and knit together by joints and ligaments, grows with the increase that is from God."*

What was Paul saying to you and me? That Christ is **the source of life** who nourishes the church. We are to hold fast to Christ who is the "head" **(Giver of LIFE)** from whom the whole body, nourished and knit together through its joints and ligaments, grows with a growth that is from GOD.

*Colossians 1:16-19: "For by Him all things were created that are in heaven and that are on earth, visible and invisible, whether thrones or dominions or principalities or powers. All things were created through Him and for Him. And He is before all things, and in Him all things consist. And **He is the head ("giver of life" of the body**, the church, **who is the beginning**, the firstborn from the dead, that in all things He may have the preeminence. For it pleased the Father that in Him all the fullness should dwell;"*

In *I Corinthians 11*, Paul was dealing with the argument for head coverings. The traditions of men were always trying to edge their way back into this newfound freedom called Christianity. Paul had to continually confront the problems of Jewish and oral laws, as much as Jesus had to deal with them.

1 Corinthians 11:16: "But if anyone seems to be contentious, <u>__we__</u> <u>__have no such custom, nor do the churches of God.__</u>"

Paul put a quick wrench in their spokes, when they were trying to get their women back to wearing head covers, and back into the law. When we understand the time, history, and the grammar it brings a better understanding of God's word. It's rich; the word of God is filled with *life, purpose, and destiny.*

Paul was saying, *"as Christ is* the *source, giver of life"* to the church, man *"is the source and giver of life"* to the woman. Man brings life to his wife, **not** "rule OVER." This is very powerful; when a man and woman understand that the husband is to love, give life, and nourish this amazing gift that God has brought to his side as his *wife.* When a man/husband understands this meaning, and acts according to God's life-giving love, it brings a heavenly peace to the home, and security to the heart of the wife. She begins to grow with a high respect and honor towards her husband. She begins to love him in a special way, and God's love begins to flow right out of heaven, like He planned from the very beginning.

This is why, when Paul describes the marriage of a husband and wife in Ephesians 5:32: "This is a great mystery, but I speak concerning Christ and the church."

The word, *"the source, the giver of life,"* needs to be understood today in the Christian marriage. When both man/woman understand this, harmony will reign in the home. Together a husband/wife become a powerful tool for God. The devil is frightened when he finds a home where God is recognized as the *"giver of life",* and love and respect are given to one another.

With this understanding both the husband and wife are equally one in Christ Jesus.

Without Christ dying on the cross, we would not have a beginning or life. Jesus, *"is the life giver to the body,"* the

Church. Adam was the beginning, *"giver of life,"* to woman. Without Adam's rib, and God's amazing handy work, we *ladies* wouldn't be. Thank God for man!

In the middle of I Corinthians Chapter 14, Paul brings up the following two verses:

I Corinthians 14:34-35: "Let your women keep silent in the churches, for they are not permitted to speak; but they are to be submissive as the law also says. And if they want to learn something, let them ask their own husbands at home; for it is shameful for women to speak in church."

Two very important ideas need to be examined here: What law is the Apostle Paul referring to when he says, "...as the law also says"? After carefully studying the law, which the Lord gave in the Old Testament books of Exodus, Leviticus, Deuteronomy and Numbers, there is *no sign* of a law that forbids women from speaking in church. Neither is there any command nor rule which says, "...it is shameful for women to speak in church." *(Once again, this portion of scripture is the Apostle Paul quoting the Talmud, the oral law."*

Paul is *not* supporting the oral law; he is only repeating what the Talmud says. When this section is taken in context, Paul goes on in verses 36-37 to bring a rebuke:

"Or did the word of God come originally from you? Or was it you only that it reached? If anyone thinks himself to be a prophet or spiritual, let him acknowledge that the things, which I write to you, are the commandments of the Lord. But if anyone is ignorant, let him be ignorant."

Second...

God does not go against His Word. The Apostle Paul was not contradicting himself; he was only wading through the mud of religious tradition. Every chapter of the book of Corinthians has Paul dealing with the fast growing church in Corinth, addressing many issues and problems in their church. The *primary* problem was that the Jews were receiving Christ and trying to merge their laws and traditions with New Testament Christianity. These men were known as the Judaizers.

You would not believe some of the explanations I have heard of this portion of the Bible. I was shocked by some very intelligent, very spiritual, and respected preachers supporting the doctrine of the Judaizers and Talmud in the church today.

In some Christian churches in the United States, women must cover their heads; in others the women must wear long dresses and no makeup. Others claim the silence of women in the church; yet they contradict themselves by allowing women to pray and sing, permitting some even to prophesy, testify, or teach Sunday school. The obvious conclusion is that religious traditions cannot be combined with the gospel of Jesus Christ. This results in confusion, contradiction, and division; these are tools of the devil.

How can this be explained, simply?

The Apostle Paul clearly writes:

Galatians 3:26-28: "For as many of you as were baptized into Christ have put on Christ. There is neither Jew nor Greek, there is neither slave nor free, there is neither male nor female; for you are all one in Christ Jesus."

GIVE THEM A POSSESSION

17

Numbers 27:7: "The daughters of Zelophehad speak what is right; you shall surely give them a possession of inheritance among their father's brothers, and cause the inheritance of their father to pass to them."

Sometimes when we see something written, it seems like there's a period, but it may not be the end. We must understand the heartbeat of God; know His love, and His compassion towards you and me. His love is far beyond the traditions, religions, and rituals. When I think about the five daughters of Zelophehad in Numbers 27:1-11, these verses speak volumes, not only to me, but they should speak to every woman who has a call of God on her life. These five women stood before the congregation, the leaders, and the priest, in a time when women were not allowed an inheritance of land. They took this problem to Moses. Even Moses was somewhat bewildered about what to do concerning these five women, but Moses took it before the Lord.

These five sisters: Mahlah, Noah, Hoglah, Milcah, and Tirzah, knew in their hearts that what was happening was unfair and not right. They knew the heartbeat of a loving heavenly Father; a Father who is fair, full of mercy, grace, and loving kindness. Because of the boldness of these five women who were willing to stand against all odds, they stood, knowing only God could change and bring understanding to the existing written law. Because they were willing to stand strong, they helped change the unfair law. God Himself spoke to Moses, telling him: "The daughters of Zelophehad speak what is right; you shall surely give them a possession of inheritance among their father's brothers, and cause the inheritance of their father to pass to them."

I stand in the love of my heavenly Father who has called me out of darkness, and brought me into His amazing service. *I'm not writing this book to change a law, but to show the difference between man's traditions, and the truth of God's word.* These *traditions* hinder and hold women captive in a wicked lie from Satan to stop God's command to "go forth and preach the gospel."

My purpose is to share the heartbeat of my God.

Many of the daughters of God have been mistreated, and are not allowed their *inheritance-* the promise- which was to be given to all people, both men and women who come to Jesus by faith, to have dominion over the earth, not one another.

❧❧❧❧❧❧❧❧❧❧❧❧❧❧❧❧❧❧❧❧❧❧❧❧❧❧❧❧

*Joel 2:28-32: "And it shall come to pass afterward that I will our out My Spirit on all flesh; your sons and your **daughters shall prophesy**, your old men shall dream dreams, your young men shall see visions. And also on My menservants and **on My maidservants I will pour out My Spirit** in those days. And I will show wonders in the heavens and in the earth: blood and fire and pillars of smoke. The sun shall be turned into darkness, and the moon into blood, before the coming of the great and awesome day of the Lord. And it shall come to pass that **whoever** calls on the name of the Lord shall be saved. For in*

*Mount Zion and in Jerusalem there shall be deliverance, as the Lord has said, among the remnant **whom** the Lord calls."*

My favorite two books are I Timothy and II Timothy. They have touched my heart for many years. The urgency of Paul asking young Timothy to come quickly, bring the parchments, knowing his death was right around the corner...

*II Timothy 4:6-9: "For I am already being poured out as a drink offering, and the time of my departure is at hand. I have fought the good fight, I have finished the race, I have kept the faith. Finally, there is laid up for me the crown of righteousness, which the Lord, the righteous Judge, will give to me on that Day, and not to me only but also **to all** who have loved His appearing."*

Paul's undying love, to get the gospel message of the *cross* out, and everything in order, all the way to the very end of his life, stirs my heart. At the very end of his life, Paul expresses his love for those who labored with him, and gives them recognition, knowing he will be killed soon.

II Timothy 4:19-22: "Greet Priscilla and Aquila, and the household of Onesiphorus. Erastus stayed in Corinth, but Trophimus I have left in Miletus sick. Do your utmost to come before winter. Eubulus greets you, as well as Pudens, Linus, Claudia, and all the brethren. The Lord Jesus Christ be with your spirit. Grace be with you. Amen.

Paul's address and farewell has always brought a tear to my heart, knowing that one day I too will meet Paul the Apostle on the other side of this life.

It saddens me as I consider that many in the churches today would think the Apostle Paul was against women in ministry, and he would tell them they had to keep silent in the church. Paul was the farthest from this belief. Was Paul really against women preachers, women pastoring a church, or women teaching men/women? NO, he was not. But Paul diligently tried to bring understanding to these manmade traditions that always hinder the work of God.

Ъ&

Paul was no stranger to deception; after all he was the one who used to kill Christians, dragging men and women to their deaths. He knew the law, the Talmud, the oral law. He knew how dangerous it was to allow any of these traditions of man to distort the *truth*.

Jesus was the same; when you read through the time Jesus walked on this earth, He was always coming to women's defense. We read these beautiful experiences:

- *The doubled-over woman in the synagogue whom He called a daughter of Abraham;*
- *The woman at the well;*
- *The woman caught in adultery;*
- *The woman washing His feet,* and the list goes on and on...

All through the life of Paul, he always gave honor and respect to women. In the books of Acts, Romans, and I Corinthians, we find greetings and acknowledgments of fellow laborers, including woman workers:

- Lydia, a convert from Thyatira, whose church was in her house, *Acts 16:14 & 16:40*
- Phoebe, a servant of the church in Cenchrea, *Romans 16:1*
- Priscilla and Aquila, fellow workers who risked their own lives for him and the church of the Gentiles, *Romans 16:3, and I Corinthians 16:19*
- Mary, who labored much for him, *Romans 16:6*
- Tryphaena, Tryphosa, and the beloved Persis, who labored for the Lord, *Romans 16:12*

- Junia, a female apostle[3], *Romans 16:7*

"John Chyrsostom (337-407), bishop of Constantintople, wasn't partial to women. He said some negative things about women but spoke positively about Junia. "Oh, how great is the devotion of this woman that she should be counted worthy of the appellation of apostle!" Nor was he the only church father to believe Junia was a woman. Origen of Alexandria (c. 185-253) said the name was a variant of Julia (Rom. 16:15), as does Thayer's Lexicon. Leonard Swidler cited Jerome (340-419), Hatto of Vercelli (924-961), Theophylack (1050-1108), and Peter Abelard (1079-1142) as believing Junia to be a woman.

Dr. Swidler stated, "To the best of my knowledge, no commentator on the text until Aegidus of Rom (1245-1316) took the name to be masculine." Apparently, the idea that Junia was a man's name is a relatively modern concept but the bulk of evidence available is that Junia was indeed a woman, and an outstanding apostle."[4]

Here is a closer look at Priscilla,[5] "The wife of Aquila, Priscilla, was a staunch supporter of Paul and a mature Christian leader in the early church. Priscilla and Aquila, as Jews, had been expelled from Rome, and lived at Corinth when Paul met them. They worked together earning their living as tentmakers and getting the small colony of Christians started. They accompanied Paul to Ephesus and stayed there when Paul traveled on to Jerusalem. *Priscilla showed herself a person of exceptional tact and maturity when she <u>corrected some of the errors</u> (teaching) in the preaching of the brilliant Apollos.* Their church in Ephesus was in their home. After the riots against Christians, they shifted to Rome again and later back to Ephesus.

"Priscilla apparently was more prominent than her husband (her name precedes her husband's in four out of the six references) although both were highly regarded as early missionaries."

If Paul really meant women should be silent in the church, then why would he say in *I Corinthians 11:5: "But every woman that **prayeth or prophesieth** with her head uncovered dishonoureth her head: for that is even all one as if she were shaven."*

Paul was not confused, about women who **prayeth or prophesieth,** not one bit. Over and over many women who have been called of God have been told, *"Read I Timothy,"* as an explanation why women could not preach.

I Timothy 2:11-15: "Let a woman learn in silence with all submission. And I do not permit a woman to teach or to have authority over a man, but to be in silence. For Adam was formed first, then Eve. And Adam was not deceived, but the woman being deceived, fell into transgression. Nevertheless she will be saved in childbearing if they continue in faith, love and holiness, with self-control."

I prayed, "Lord, reveal to me these verses." The same method to study the Bible is needed to clarify the meaning of these verses: the context, history, and grammar. There is *no* contradiction in Paul's instructions. Contradiction occurs only when verses are taken out of context.

What is the context of these verses in I Timothy?

*I Timothy 1:3-4: "As I urged you when I went into Macedonia remain in Ephesus that you may charge some that they **teach no other doctrine**, nor give heed to fables and endless genealogies, which cause disputes rather than godly edification which is in the faith."*

According to *Commentary Critical and Explanatory on the Whole Bible*[6], other groups were bringing false doctrines into the New Testament churches; in this case it was the Judaizers and the Gnostics. Gnostics believed that when Adam and Eve ate of the fruit in Genesis, they had "special knowledge,"-*gnosis*. The church in Ephesus had trouble with a group of Gnostic women. These women were using sexuality to lure men to follow their false teaching in the church. This explains:

I Timothy 2:9: "...in like manner also, that the women adorn themselves in modest apparel, with propriety and moderation, not with braided hair or gold or pearls or costly clothing, but, which is proper for women professing godliness, with good works."

These Gnostic women were opposite of this description, their apparel was not modest, and their behavior was not godly. **Their pagan religion** included a belief of joining their flesh with the "spirit," in sexual acts of worship. Ephesus was a city filled with sexual immorality and temple prostitutes.[7] When the Apostle Paul goes on in the next verse, he is referring to the Gnostic women:

I Timothy 2:11: "Let a woman learn in silence with all submission."

Paul used, "authentein", which meant "sexual license". The sexual nature of their teaching is revealed in the next verse during the time period in which Paul wrote the letter to Timothy. ***Over two hundred years after Paul wrote to Timothy, the meaning was changed to mean, "to usurp authority."***

I Timothy 2:12: "And I do not permit a woman to teach or to have authority ("authentein") over a man, but to be in silence."

Paul did not permit these women to teach using their "sexual license" over a man.

The context is continued in the next two verses of this chapter because Paul is still referring to the false teaching of Gnosticism regarding Adam and Eve, and their beliefs of having special power.

I Timothy 2:13-14: "For Adam was formed first, then Eve. And Adam was not deceived, but the woman being deceived, fell into transgression."

Paul was disproving the Gnostic claim that Eve received "special knowledge," when she ate the fruit. Instead, when she ate the fruit, she was deceived and fell into transgression. It is Paul's simple warning against their **false doctrine;** Gnosticism is deception and leads to sin!

The final verse at face value has been troublesome, **unless** you continue with Paul's teaching in context:

I Timothy 2:15: "Nevertheless she will be saved in childbearing if they continue in faith, love, and holiness, with self-control."

Who was saved in childbearing? **Eve!** Through childbearing, *eventually* the promised **_Seed,_** Jesus, would fulfill God's promise from *Genesis 3:15*. Salvation would come through Christ.

Notice how the grammar changes from "she" to "they" in the same verse. If "they," the Gnostic women, continue in faith, love and holiness, with self-control, they too can be saved.

The verses in *I Timothy* **do not** support a doctrine against women in the ministry. Once again, Paul is teaching that those caught in the web of false doctrine can come to the truth and salvation through Christ Jesus and be saved. If these Gnostic women learn to dress modestly, learn in silence with all submission, they too can be saved from sin.

It saddens me deeply that many twist the Bible, which is to bring life and freedom, yet is being used to prevent women from fulfilling their purpose in God's kingdom, because of the lack of understanding.

When Jesus bruised the head of Satan, the curse was broken. As joint heirs with Christ, we **all** *have* **been** restored to God's promises from the beginning. The curse is broken!

What is the conclusion? Can a woman be called of God? Can a woman preach? Can a woman teach? Can a woman lead? Yes! Yes! Yes! Yes! The Lord has always used women and men to establish and build His kingdom from the Old Testament to the New Testament.

In Judges, Chapter 4, Deborah was a prophetess, the wife of Lapidoth and the judge of Israel. God used ***her as the leader*** of the nation of Israel. In war, she commanded Barak to take troops to destroy the enemy. He would not go without her. Then God used another woman, Jael, to kill the enemy, as a fulfillment of Deborah's prophecy, that the Lord would deliver Sisera into the hand of a woman.

The list includes Esther, who saved the Hebrews out of the hand of the enemy in the book of Esther. Then there is Anna, the ***prophetess,*** in *Luke 2:36,* who served in the temple with fasting and prayers night and day.

The Samaritan woman at the well, in *John 4,* who received Christ and went to her city to tell them all that Jesus had said to her. In *Acts 21,* Phillip the evangelist had four virgin daughters who prophesied. *Prophesying is giving a message from God, teaching and preaching.*

Throughout history, God has called women into the ministry. I am sure that each one, with a story of brokenness and great challenges, stepped forward to the command of her God.

Following is a *very* small list of some well-known women of God; and there are many other women whose names are not written and known only in heaven. Despite opposition, trials and prejudice, many women have and will continue to faithfully fulfill God's mission of *Mark 16:15*: "Go forth and preach the gospel to every living creature, and lo, I will be with you always."

Maria Woodworth-Etter: (July 22, 1844-September 16, 1924) Within a short time after Maria Woodworth-Etter responded to God's call to "go out in the highways and hedges and gather in the lost sheep", people were thronging to hear her speak with signs and wonders following. By 1885, without a public address system, crowds of over twenty-five thousand pressed in to hear her minister, while hundreds fell to the ground under the power of God. Woodworth-Etter not only shook up denominational religion, she rocked the secular world with life-altering displays of God's power.

Those who came to investigate, condemn, or harass her seemed most at risk of "falling out" in what was described as a trancelike state. Maria preached that these strong manifestations of the Spirit were "nothing new; they were just something the Church had lost." She was unwavering in her determination to break the strongholds that held people, communities, and whole cities in bondage. It seemed the more opposition she faced, the more she dug in her heels. Maria produced invincible strength through tenacious prayer, enabling her to take authority and minister with grace and power. She was known as a revivalist who could break towns open.

Aimee Semple McPherson: (October 9, 1890-September 27, 1944), also known as Sister Aimee. She founded the Foursquare Church. McPherson has been noted as a pioneer in the use of modern media, especially radio, and was the second woman t o be granted a broadcast license. She used radio to reach thousands for Jesus Christ. She also built Angelus Temple in Los Angeles, still being used for God today. A powerful woman called of God, Sister Aimee not only preached, but trained and launched out thousands of men and women to preach the gospel throughout the world. Her Legacy,

International Church of the Foursquare Gospel, continues into the entire WORLD today.

Kathryn Kuhlman: (May 9, 1907-February 20, 1976) was an American faith healer and evangelist, who was used by God powerfully to touch thousands of lives. Kathryn Johanna Kuhlman was born in Concordia, Missouri, to German-American parents. She was "born-again" at the age of 14 in the Methodist Church of Concordia, and began preaching in the West at the age of sixteen in primarily Baptist Churches.

Kuhlman traveled extensively around the United States and in many other countries holding "healing crusades" between the 1940s and 1970s. She had a weekly TV program in the 1960s and 1970s called I Believe In Miracles that was aired nationally. The foundation was established in 1954, and its Canadian branch in 1970.[8]

Marilyn Hickey: (born July 1, 1931- still going strong), a powerful pastor, and teacher, who also ministers on television, has traveled the globe, and has seen thousands come to Jesus Christ.

Her husband, the late Wallace Hickey, challenged her commitment to Christ and was her encouragement to become a Pentecostal. They founded Full Gospel Chapel in Denver. This church, know as Orchard Road Christian Center, is now one of the largest churches in the Denver area, and currently meets in a former mall in Greenwood Village. Over 80 years old and still ministering, this amazing woman of God has imparted the vision and purpose of God into their daughter, ***Sarah Bowling, who with her husband, Reece***, has taken over the pastorate for her. Her ministry continues on.

A very special thanks to the late Wallace Hickey, for his never ending support of his wife and daughter, your reward I'm sure was fantastic in heaven.

<u>Joyce Meyer:</u> (June 4, 1943- present) is another powerful woman called of God. An author and speaker, Joyce and her husband Dave have four grown children, and live outside St. Louis, Missouri. Her ministry is headquartered in the St. Louis suburb of Fenton, Missouri. She began leading an early-morning Bible class at a local cafeteria and became active in Life Christian Center, a charismatic church in Fenton. Within a few years, Meyer was the church's associate pastor. The church became one of the leading charismatic churches in the area, largely because of her popularity as a Bible teacher. She also began airing a daily 15-minute radio broadcast on a St. Louis radio station.

In 1985, Joyce founded her own ministry called "Life in the Word." She began airing her radio show on six other stations from Chicago to Kansas City. In 1993, her husband Dave suggested that they start a television ministry. Initially airing on superstation WGN-TV in Chicago and Black Entertainment Television (BET), her program, now called "Enjoying Everyday Life", is still on the air today, reaching millions with the gospel of Jesus Christ.

A special thank you to Dave Meyer, for supporting Joyce, and your wife's calling, so millions of both men and women can be saved.

<u>Daisy Marie Washburn Osborn</u>, the wife of the late, TL Osborn. Osborn married Daisy Washburn Osborn at the age of 17, and shortly thereafter the two together set out on a life of ministry and missionary travel with a trip to India at the age of 21. By the early 1950s their emphasis began to shift more and more toward efforts in international missions. They began to hold large crusades in Latin America, Asia, and Africa where crowds began to grow rapidly and at times reached well over 100,000 persons in attendance in a single meeting. These crusades at times began to have a very significant impact on cities, provinces, and sometimes even whole nations. Osborn's crusades in Thailand in 1956 and Uganda in 1957 for instance are said to have laid the foundations for substantial growth in Pentecostalism in those countries. Over the course of the next 5 decades the team traveled to more than 70 countries and reached millions of people. They created prolific quantities of missionary evangelism and training materials, some of which have now been translated into more than 80 languages. Daisy precedes her husband in death May 1995. Yet this ministry continues to travel and conduct crusades around the world. Dr. T.L. Osborn died in his mid-eighties on February 14, 2013 at the age of 89. Today Osborn's daughter

Ladonna Osborn continues to operate the ministry founded by her parents, including leading international crusades in the developing world every year.[9]

Anne Graham – Lotz, (born May 21, 1948) is an American Christian evangelist. She is the second daughter of evangelist Billy Graham and his wife Ruth Graham. She founded AnGeL Ministries, and is the author of 11 books, of which her best known is *Just Give Me Jesus.*[10]

A powerful woman of God, and a great example to many.

Many women, called of God, preach today, unknown by anyone on this earth, but their names are known in heaven. Many women throughout the world right now preach throughout the nations of Africa, Pakistan, Iran, China, Russia, and many third world countries. Knowing very well that they may be caught and killed for their faith in Jesus, they willingly accept the call to preach. Why? Because of the love and freedom Jesus brought to them.

Many women today have given their lives to preach the gospel of Jesus Christ. Many women today are in prisons throughout the world, alone, broken, beaten, raped, and tormented for preaching the gospel message of Jesus Christ in Muslim communities who dominate women by an evil god of the Koran, where women are considered mere property.

May the Holy Spirit help you who read this book- whether you are a man or woman, to know- *together we can make a great impact for Jesus...**together,*** we can change the world we live in, but only through the gospel message being preached for Jesus Christ, our Lord and Savior.

With a population rising to 7 billion: sin rising, and Satan fervently working nonstop to gather people into hell, God needs His army. Not just half of His army is needed; He is calling both men and women into His service.

Dr. David Yonggi Cho, I had the privilege to see and be a part of the most amazing church in the world. God has used this man to build the largest Christian church in the world. Dr. David Yonggi Cho has understood the value of women. He has released women, and they work today, side by side, to build the kingdom of God as a stronghold in Seoul, Korea.

Dr. Cho has made this compellingly powerful statement: "Until America learns to release their women, they will never have revival in their land." I was honored to have this man, Dr. David Yonggi Cho, pray for me, and anoint me for the work God had called me to fulfill in America today.

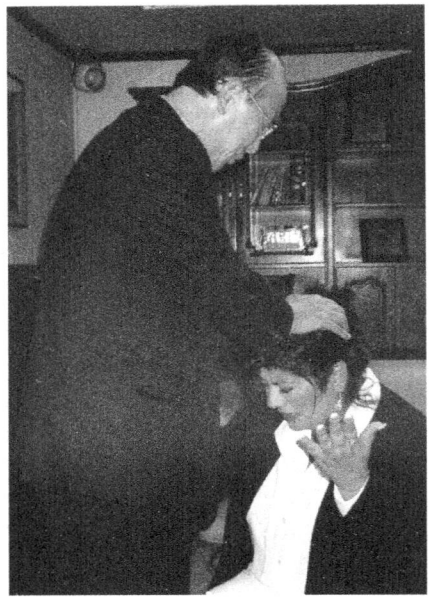

Dr. David Yonggi Cho praying for Dr. Luauna Stines

Today, I know many great men of God who recognize this *truth* and have stood strong to defend women in ministry. I want to personally thank **_Dr. Charles Trombley_**, the author of the book, *"Who Said Women Can't Teach?"* An authoritative, amazing eye opener that brings *truth* to light of what God's word says about women. I will forever be grateful to him, and his wonderful wife and great minister of the gospel, Gladys, for their words and friendship.

The International Church of the Foursquare Gospel, who train and recognize women in their leadership position in the body of Christ, thank you **President Glenn Burris**, and Pastors Joel and Kathie Phillips; their parents, Pastors, Dr. Coleman (Deceased) and Mary Phillips of Escondido Christian Center.

Pastor Jerry Dirmann founder and Senior Pastor of The Rock, a multi-congregational church based in Anaheim, CA., and his wife, **Pastor Kimberly Dirmann**, the Supervisor of the Southwest District Foursquare. And so many others...Thank you.

Matthew 28:19-20: "Go therefore and make disciples of all nation, baptizing them in the name of the Father and of the Son and of the Holy Spirit, teaching them to observe all things that I have commanded you; and lo, I am with you always event o the end of the age. Amen."

From the day I drove out of the state of Oregon with a broken heart, broken promises, and a life that was shattered into a million pieces, my heavenly Father saw me, and picked me up.

Yes! --- I *was* wrong, and I take full responsibility for my actions; I should have never gotten married "so I could go preach." (Chapter 10) I created an Ishmael, and paid dearly for it.

Yes! --- I was wrong to allow anybody but Jesus Christ, my Lord and Savior, to have control in the destiny of my spiritual life.

It has been 18 years from the day when I left Oregon, to the day I write this book. No, I am not remarried. Will I ever get married? I don't know- maybe yes, maybe no. One thing I do know is my heavenly Father knows my calling, and my heartbeat is to do His will, to reach a lost and dying world for Him. If my heavenly Father desires for me to marry, then He will bring that amazing, "Life giver," to my side, and he will love me, and know, I am *"A Woman Called of God."* If I never marry, I am complete in Christ Jesus, and I will continue to fulfill His call on my life.

Today as I write this book, I have been saved for 35 years; *I am a woman called of God;* I am free to be all the Lord wants me to be, and I have removed the invisible *head burqa.* The choice is to obey Jesus, my Lord and Savior.

Who am I? I am no one special. Just like a small potato in a great big potato patch, just doing my part in God's wonderfully *amazing, big* kingdom on this earth. Will I convince everyone that women can preach? Probably not!

Joel 2:25-27: "And I will restore to you the years that the locust hath eaten, the cankerworm, and the caterpillar, and the palmerworm, my great army which I sent among you. And ye shall eat in plenty, and be satisfied, and praise the name of the Lord your God, that hath dealt wondrously with you: and my people shall never be ashamed. And ye shall know that I am in the midst of Israel, and that I am the Lord your God, and none else: and my people shall never be ashamed."

<u>As of today, I am preparing an online, "A Touch from Above-Christian University"</u> to train and equip, millions of both men and women for the purpose of preaching the gospel of Jesus Christ to a world lost and perishing in darkness.

I minister on radio every Sunday morning in San Diego, California, and on television twice a week. By God's wonderful grace, I have purchased 25 acres, in the heart of San Diego County. We are building a Christian Prayer Mountain, dedicated for God's people to pray and fast, that they too might find God's perfect will for their lives.

Number 27:6-7: "And the Lord spake unto Moses, saying, the daughters of Zelophehad speak right: thou shalt surely give them a possession of an inheritance among their father's brethren; and though shalt cause the inheritance of their father to pass unto them."

Women of God! Rise up and take your *inheritance! God bless you, and know, I love you, I'm praying for you, and-*

I Am A Woman Called Of God

COLORADO SPRINGS, COLORADO
DR. LUAUNA STINES, WITNESSING TO BIKERS

DENVER, COLORADO
DR. LUAUNA STINES ON STATE CAPITOL

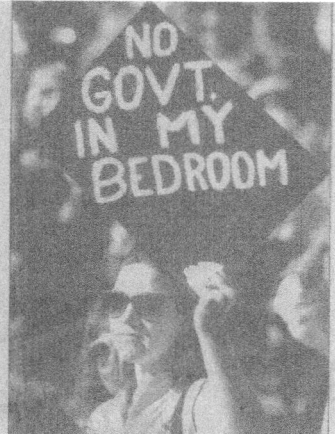

ANOTHER VIEW: Luauna Stines holds a Bible during counterprotest of abortion rights rally at state Capitol.

CHOICE: Katie Betts waves pro-choice sign at same rally attended by about 500 people yesterday.

Pro-choice backers flex muscles

Wirth tells 500 at rally most Americans favor abortion rights

By Pat McGraw
Denver Post Staff Writer

Colorado abortion activists kicked off their part of "the largest pro-choice effort in American history" yesterday, vowing to be heard over the strident voices of their anti-abortion counterparts.

U.S. Sen. Tim Wirth, D-Colo., told a gathering of about 500 people at the state Capitol that the majority of America is pro-choice.

As proof, Wirth cited this week's elections in New York City, New Jersey and Virginia, where pro-choice candidates beat their anti-abortion foes.

And although recent votes in the U.S. House and Senate indicate that pro-choice sentiment is being heeded, Wirth

■ **OPERATION RESCUE:** Crowd protests outside doctor's office./3B

said it will take continued, organized effort to assure that "the shrill, marginal types no longer dominate this debate."

The rally was the first in a week-long schedule of pro-choice activities, which include a gathering at East 17th Avenue and York Street at 9 a.m. and a march and rally at 10 a.m. in Boulder today.

Pro-choice forces will march on Washington today in what is expected to be one of the largest pro-choice rallies to date.

Four Colorado state senators and 16 state representatives also were on the

Capitol steps to endorse the effort. One of several speakers among them, Sen. Dottie Wham, R-Denver, said an abortion decision is "a matter of personal concern, not that of the government." State Rep. Pat Pascoe, D-Denver, blasted University of Colorado football coach Bill McCartney's support of anti-abortionists: "He would order women to have children, no matter what the circumstances."

The 55-minute gathering also attracted a handful of anti-abortion partisans. Luauna Stines of Colorado Springs alternatively sang gospel numbers and quoted scripture at one corner of the unreceptive crowd.

The rally ended without confrontation.

SEOUL, SOUTH KOREA
DR. DAVID YONGGI CHO & DR. LUAUNA STINES

SEOUL, SOUTH KOREA
DR. LUAUNA STINES PREACHING WITH INTERPRETER PASTOR LEE HAE KYU

CORVALLIS, OREGON
DR. LUAUNA STINES, OUTREACH AT CITY HALL, NARAL RALLY

MALAWI, CENTRAL AFRICA
DR. LUAUNA STINES PREACHING WITH INTERPRETER IN THE VILLAGE

RAMONA, CALIFORNIA
FLIGHT LESSONS FOR EMERGENCY FLIGHT OUT OF AFRICA BUSH

SAN DIEGO, CALIFORNIA
DR. LUAUNA STINES, PETCO PARK
OUTSIDE CHURCH SERVICE

COSTA MESA, CALIFORNIA
TRINITY BROADCASTING NETWORK STUDIOS
DR. LUAUNA STINES SPEAKER
FOR SOUL WINNING CONFERENCE

RAMONA, CALIFORNIA
EVANGELIST, DR. LUAUNA STINES
IN SPANISH CHURCH –

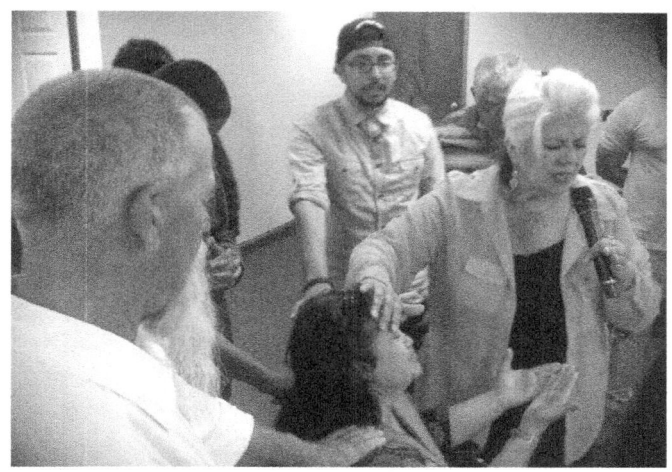

SAN DIEGO, CALIFORNIA
DR. LUAUNA STINES WITH DR. JAMES DOBSON, FAMILY TALK RADIO

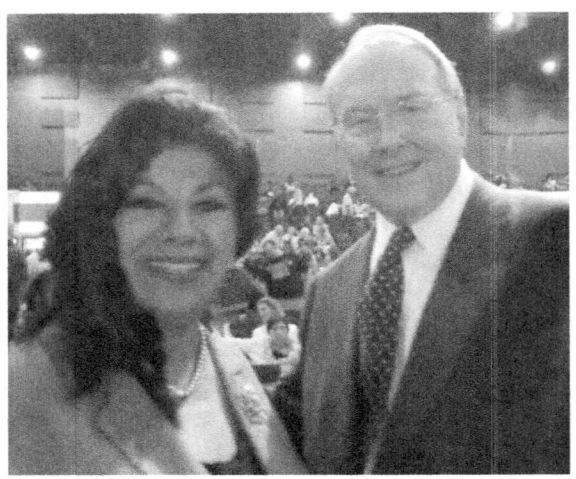

RAMONA, CALIFORNIA
DR. LUAUNA STINES, FILMING TELEVISION PROGRAM FOR SAN DIEGO, CALIFORNIA

La Jolla, California
Dr. Luauna Stines Preaching on Radio
KPRZ 1210 AM – reaching all of San Diego

RAMONA, CALIFORNIA
DR. LUAUNA STINES PREACHING
AT PRAYER MOUNTAIN

RAMONA, CALIFORNIA

RAMONA, CALIFORNIA
A TOUCH FROM ABOVE – PRAYER MOUNTAIN
DR. LUAUNA STINES, PREACHING SUNDAY SERVICE

SAN DIEGO, CALIFORNIA
A TOUCH FROM ABOVE
CHURCH ON THE BEACH

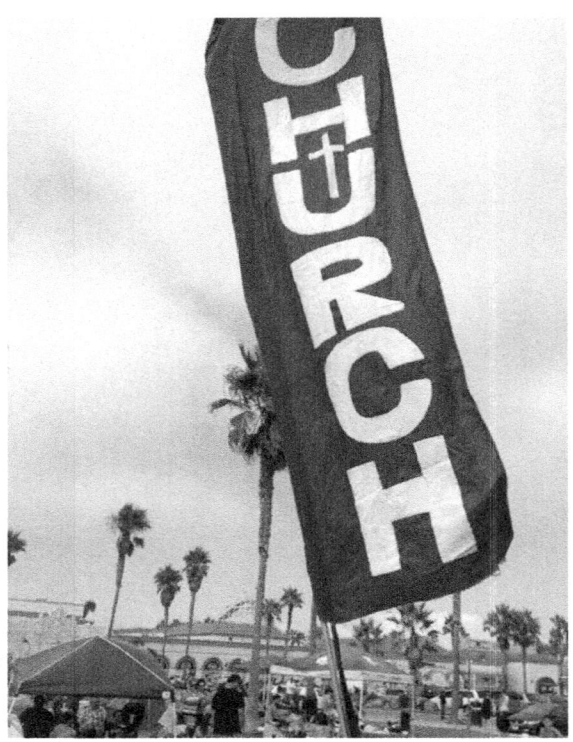

ANAHEIM, CALIFORNIA
AT THE ROCK CHURCH
DR. LUAUNA STINES PREACHING

ANAHEIM, CALIFORNIA
THE ROCK CHURCH

SAN DIEGO, CALIFORNIA
DINESH D'SOUZA & DR. LUAUNA STINES
New York Times Bestselling Author & Filmmaker
The movies: *2016* & *America-Imagine A World Without Her*

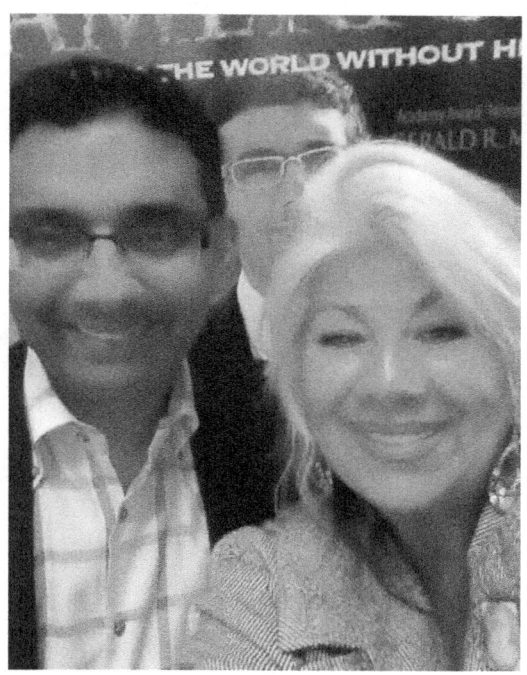

SAN DIEGO, CALIFORNIA
A TOUCH FROM ABOVE – OUR MISSION AMERICA, "ONE NATION UNDER GOD"

www.atouchfromabove.org

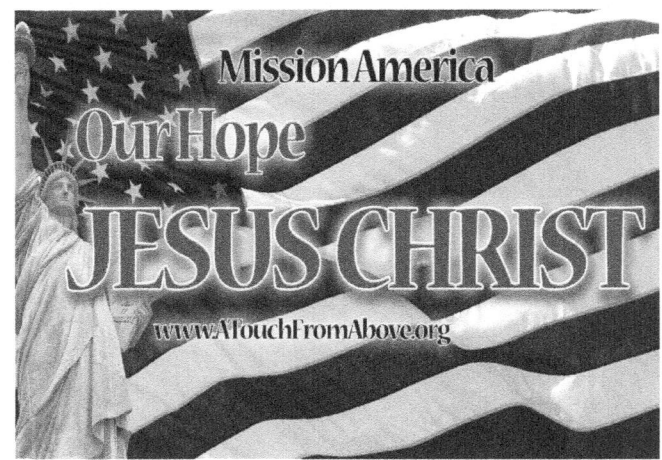

TO BOOK DR. LUAUNA STINES

ATouchFromAbove.org

760-789-6207

CONNECT WITH DR. LUAUNA STINES

Facebook: Dr. Luauna Stines

Facebook: A Touch From Above Prayer Mountain

Twitter: @DrLuaunaStines

YouTube: Dr. Luauna Stines

Write Dr. Luauna Stines-P.O Box 2800 –Ramona, CA 92065

Email: PastorLuauna@ATouchFromAbove.org

Email: DrLuauna@ATouchFromAbove.org

OTHER BOOKS BY DR. LUAUNA STINES

A Mother's Story: Available on Kindle and Paperback copyright © 2013

My story, read how my life was torn about, the death of a husband, betrayal of marriage and a trap of drugs.

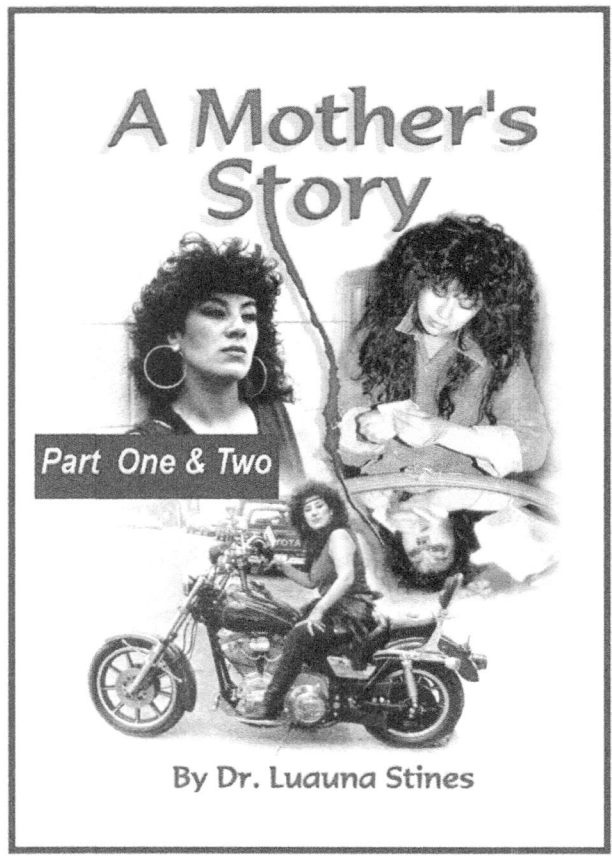

Golden Nuggets: Available on Kindle and Paperback
copyright © 2013

When someone discovers gold, it's a treasure with great value, and something to be cherished. Wisdom comes with counsel, and many times wisdom is hidden away in words and in the written word. In these pages are Golden Nuggets, wisdom which money can't buy, and is much more valuable than money. These are true stories. Glean and value what you read, it can be life to your soul.

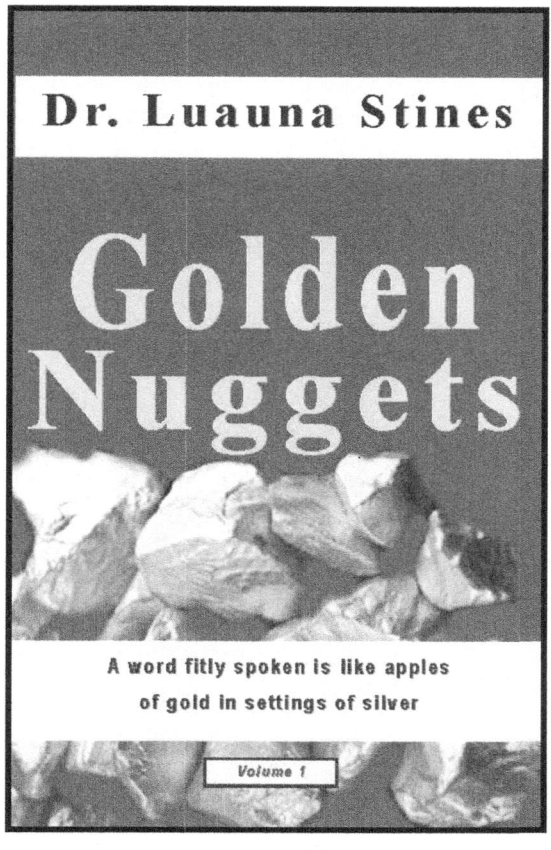

Mission America: Available on Kindle and Paperback
copyright © 2012

A true story of faith, five single women traveled across the United States of America with 250,000 gospel tracts, a gospel tent and Bibles. Starting from San Diego, CA to the East Coast preaching in every stop and every town; then home again. Reloaded and up the coast of California to Washington state, and throughout the Western United States. Hundreds and thousands of lives were touched and changed by the power of the Lord.

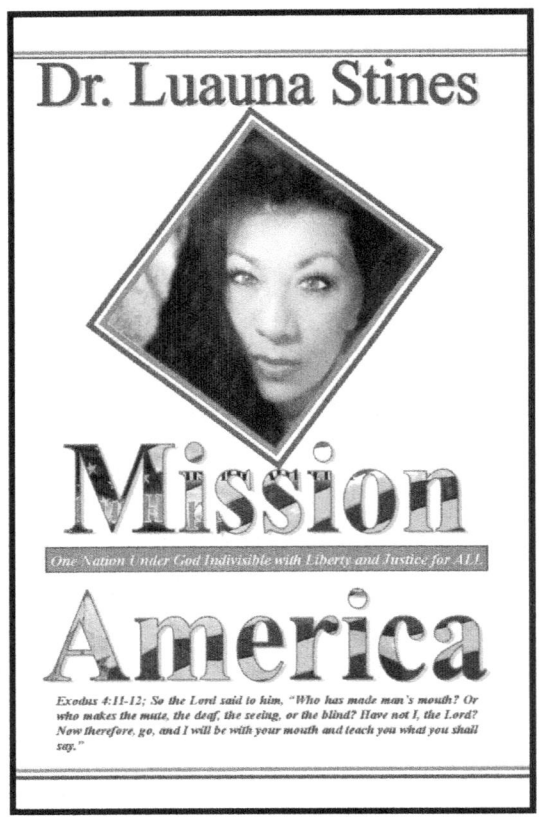

UPCOMING TITLES

BORN FOR GREATNESS copyright © 2014

Learn how to fulfill your potential. Live how God planned. You are created in the image of God. You have been destined for greatness! Why live below? Rise up! Settle for nothing less than God's best!

COME ON IN copyright © 2014

"Come on in and discover the REAL TRUE LIGHT! The world is filled with many counterfeit and deceptive ideas a façade of the Light. Don't be fooled!

LUST THE DESTROYER copyright © 2014

The world is saturated with perversion! Are you struggling with sexual sin? Do you know someone who is? Overcome lust before it destroys YOU!

GOD'S WOMEN OF POWER copyright © 2014

Do the traditions of man keep you from reaching your full potential? God still uses women, read about this generation, the unsung heroes that are still laying hands on the sick, casting out the devils and raising the dead, women of power and anointing! "...of whom the world was not worthy." Hebrews 11:38

MIRACLE AFTER MIRACLE copyright © 2014

You will laugh, cry, and grow in faith...as I share one miracle after another. The Lord is right in our midst; He wants to perform your miracle.

PRAYER, IT WORKS copyright © 2014

Be motivated to pray like never before. Find the key to seeing your prayers answered right before your eyes! Transform the world around you!

SINGLE MOTHER, YOU'RE NOT ALONE copyright © 2014

Single mother, you are not alone! You can make it! Your dreams can come to pass for you and your children. Jesus is your Husband.

ENDNOTES:

[1] Liddel, Scott, Jones, and McKenzie *A Greek-English Lexicon*, ninth edition, (Clarendon Press, 1940).

[2] Bauer, Arndt, and Gingrich, *A Greek-English Lexicon of the New Testament* (Chicago: Uuniversity of Chicago Press, 1958).

[3] Thayer, Joseph, *Greek-English Lexicon of the New Testament* (Zondervan Publishing House, Grand Rapids, Michigan, 1968, page 306).

[4] Trombley, Charles, *Who Said Women Can't Teach?* (Bridge Publishing Inc., Plainfield, New Jersey, 1985, pages 190-191).

[5] Barker, William, *Everyone In The Bible* (Fleming H. Revell Company, Westwood, New Jersey, 1966).

[6] Jamieson, Fausset, & Brown, Commentary Critical and Explanatory on the Whole Bible (Zondervan Publishing House, Grand Rapids, Michigan page 400-401).

[7] Trombley, Charles, Who *Said Women Can't Teach?* (Bridge Publishing Inc., Plainfield, New Jersey, 1985, pages 176-178).

[8] Kathryn Kuhlman. (2014, June 29). In Wikipedia, The Free Encyclopedia. Retrieved 22:02, July 4, 2014, from http://en.wikipedia.org/w/index.php?title=Kathryn_Kuhlman&oldid=614829748

[9] T. L. Osborn. (2014, June 29). In Wikipedia, The Free Encyclopedia. Retrieved 22:02, July 4, 2014, from http://en.wikipedia.org/w/index.php?title=T._L._Osborn&oldid=614890399

[10] Anne Graham Lotz. (2014, May 12). In Wikipedia, The Free Encyclopedia. Retrieved 22:03, July 4, 2014, from http://en.wikipedia.org/w/index.php?title=Anne_Graham_Lotz&oldid=608213505

Made in the USA
Monee, IL
28 June 2023

37667820R00134